GOD, ARE YOU THERE?

Understanding God's Character and How He Interacts With Us

Bruce Hartley

GROUND TRUTH PRESS

NASHUA, NEW HAMPSHIRE

God, Are You There?:
Understanding God's Character and How He Interacts With Us

Copyright © 2018 Bruce Hartley

Published by:
GROUND TRUTH PRESS
P. O. Box 7313
Nashua, NH 03060-7313

All rights reserved. No part of this publication may be reproduced, stored in a retrieval system, or transmitted in any form by any means—electronic, mechanical, photocopy, recording, scanning, or otherwise—except for brief quotations in critical reviews or articles, without the prior written permission of the publisher, and except as provided by USA copyright law.

I have tried to recreate events, locales, and conversations from my memories of them. In order to maintain their anonymity in some instances I have changed the names of individuals and places. I may have changed some identifying characteristics and details such as physical properties, occupations, and places of residence.

Editor: Bonnie Lyn Smith
Cover design: Rob Williams
Photographer: Missi Kalma Photography

First printing 2018
Printed in the United States of America

Scripture quotations taken from the New American Standard Bible® (NASB), Copyright © 1960, 1962, 1963, 1968, 1971, 1972, 1973, 1975, 1977, 1995 by The Lockman Foundation. Used by permission. www.Lockman.org

Bold references in Scripture are my own emphases.

Trade paperback ISBN-13: 978-0-9908303-6-8
Trade paperback ISBN-10: 0-9908303-6-5

```
Publisher's Cataloging-In-Publication Data
(Prepared by The Donohue Group, Inc.)

Names: Hartley, Bruce, 1955-
Title: God, are you there? : understanding God's character and how He interacts
    with us / Bruce Hartley.
Description: Nashua, New Hampshire : Ground Truth Press, [2018] | Includes
    bibliographical references.
Identifiers: ISBN 9780990830368 (trade paperback) | ISBN 0990830365 (trade
    paperback) | ISBN 9780990830375 (ebook)
Subjects: LCSH: God (Christianity)--Knowableness. | God (Christianity)--Love. |
    God (Christianity)--Will. | Spirituality.
Classification: LCC BT103 .H37 2018 (print) | LCC BT103 (ebook) | DDC 231.042--
    dc23
```

2018936404

DEDICATION

This book is dedicated to my brother Brian,

who left us far too soon.

I still miss you, bro,

and I can't wait to see you again in heaven!

ACKNOWLEDGMENTS

I would like to extend my deepest gratitude to all who have contributed to my life and to all who made this book possible. I hope I have made you proud with this effort. Thanks to my manuscript readers: Shirley Hartley and Natalie Kalma, and to my editor, Bonnie Lyn Smith, whose encouragement and guidance have proven invaluable in all aspects of this undertaking. Thanks also to Missi Kalma for her flattering photograph and to our cover designer, Rob Williams, and to many others who offered their opinions and advice.

I would like to extend a special thanks to all those who have taught God's Word to me, especially to those pastors whose teaching I have had the privilege to sit under: Raymer Matson, Alex Ayers, Phil Truesdale, Ted Nissen, David Ruff, Bob Lehleitner, Tom Ryan, Ernie Gruen, Tom Blasco, David Busic, Dave Thornhill, Richard Lauby, Densel Ball, Matt Maestas, Jeremy Krause, David Robinson, Marty Burch, Neil Bilyeu, Craig Nienaber, and Cody Waterman. Our pastors are a treasured resource, and we should never take them for granted.

Finally, many thanks to my Lord, Jesus Christ. I hope I have honored You with this work and with my life. Thank You for not abandoning me to my own devices, and thank You for never giving up on me.

Hallelujah!

TABLE OF CONTENTS

Preface ix
1 The Unexamined Life 1
2 Mercy Finds Us 9
3 Knowing God 17
4 The Question of Good and Evil 25
5 The Nature of Faith 35
6 Prayer: The Bridge to Faith 47
7 The Author of Faith 59
8 God of Love and God of Judgment 65
9 Can We Rely on God to Take Care of Us? 75
10 Is God Trustworthy? 89
11 How Do We Know God Loves Us? 103
12 Theology and a Little Dust in the Wind 119
13 How to Determine God's Will for Your Life 125
14 Do We Have the Right to Judge Others? 137
15 Is the Bible True? 145
16 Distinguishing Between Punishment and Discipline ... 155
17 The Art of Thankful Service 161
18 Positive Suffering 167
Epilogue 173
Notes 175

Preface

WHAT IS TRUTH? Your answer to such an admittedly weighty question probably depends in part upon your frame of reference. As a baby boomer who came of age in the mid-to-late 1970s, there was no gold standard of truth for my generation. We questioned seemingly everything—most acutely, our parent's values. In terms of spirituality, it was a supermarket of confections, including any and all flavors, everything from transcendental meditation to personal development movements like the "self-actualization" EST (Erhard Seminars Training) seminars. "If you don't like one, try another" seemed to be the course we prescribed for ourselves. The religious mores of our parents were left groping for a foothold as we experimented with drugs, "free" love (we found out nothing was free—most of all, love), more drugs, and anything else we deemed worth trying on for size.

One of the things inadvertently left in the dust of our experimentation was truth. We certainly held ourselves to no explicit standard of behavior, or else we would have been labeled as "uptight" by our peers. Very seldom did anyone mention "God" in my circle of friends. The thought of being told what to do or what to believe was anathema to us. We were free spirits, held in tow by no one and subject to no power greater than ourselves.

However, we overlooked the fact that truth, by its very definition, is not generational, nor is it subject to any one person's relative interpretation based on their individual preferences. For that matter, even collective agreement does not certify what is or isn't true. The truth will always be just that: the truth. Our "beliefs," whatever they may be, do not have the power to change truth. I can look you in the eye and tell you I don't believe in gravity, but tomorrow morning when I get out of bed, my feet are going to hit the floor and stick to it. The truth is a singular, exclusive thing, for which the evidence proffered should be incontrovertible.

So then, "what is truth"? Those exact words were uttered by Pontius Pilate, Governor of Judea (location: present-day Israel), as Jesus stood before him awaiting judgment. You can find an account of this event in the Bible in the Gospel of John, chapter 18. Pilate's truth question was in response to this statement from Jesus:

> "...and for this I have come into the world, to testify to **the truth**. Everyone who is of **the truth** hears My voice." (John 18:37b)

But who was this man Jesus anyway, talking big, claiming to be the representative of truth? He also said this:

> "I am the way, and **the truth**, and the life; no one comes to the Father but through Me...." (John 14:6)

That's a pretty bold statement for a lowly carpenter from Nazareth, Israel, to be making.

For those of you who don't believe in God, or Jesus, or an afterlife (or the existence of the supernatural in general), please bear with me. Please indulge me for these few pages as I share some ideas and experiences. I only ask that you consider the evidence presented of a life lived—from my perspective anyway—*with* God, rather than without Him. Everyone has reasons for believing or not believing, and what follows is not an indictment of your worldview nor an attempt to violate your will, but merely a proposal, a "proof," so to speak, offered as evidence of the existence of a relationship between the Creator and the creature.

Your own perspective may differ. Perhaps you consider the Bible to be nothing more than a collection of fairy tales or fables—or equivalent to something on the level of historical fiction. You might feel that science precludes the possibility of the existence of God. Some of us were raised in a religious home and resent having those ideas forced upon us by our parents or caretakers. I had minimal exposure to religion as a child, and when I finally decided to explore the possibility of the existence of God, it was in desperation, as a last resort. I didn't have any better options available at the time, or I probably would have gone down a different road. I was a card-carrying skeptic, who had long ago dismissed religion out-of-hand as pointless ritual and meaningless verbiage, and that was the front I presented to people.

You can imagine my surprise, then, when God introduced Himself to me in a very powerful way one April day in 1982. That was the most startling day of my life because nothing in my life up to that point had come remotely close to satisfying that deep, remote emptiness I often felt—the kind that leaves you with that vaguely queasy, almost-sinking feeling when it's only you alone with your thoughts, with nothing to distract you but the silence. Perhaps you can identify with that feeling.

What follows is an exploration of what I believe Jesus was getting at in regards to truth. These are my thoughts on some of the big questions we need to answer for ourselves, and hopefully this discussion will stimulate you to go out in search of your own answers—in search of the truth.

1
THE UNEXAMINED LIFE

Depending on your perspective, our present-day culture is either moving forward too slowly—that is, we need better, faster internet load times and easier access to information and networks—or, at the other extreme, we feel everything is moving too fast. With the click of a button we can hop on or off our social networks and simultaneously disseminate and/or absorb whatever information we wish. Seemingly, our lives have become inextricably bound up with our electronic devices.

Some of us are very comfortable having all this "stuff" so easily accessible and instantly updated, since, after all, that seems to be the norm, but others struggle to avoid sensory overload as the world around them seems to be changing and mutating at an ever-astonishing speed. Unfortunately, our networking prowess has also engendered what some would say is an overall decline in the quality of communication in general. In an effort to keep pace with our booming technology, we've adopted a peculiar kind of "shortcut" approach to life—one where we don't focus on any one thing in too much detail lest we miss out on the latest thing, which purports to be an even better version of the last thing we had.

Honestly, how much time do we spend discussing our phones, looking into our phones, texting on our phones, laughing at our phones, and fiddling with our phones? We're very intimate with our phones. Some of us are our phones. But in the process are we losing the ability to hold a simple conversation exercising the skill of active listening? At times, it seems as if our culture is suffering from collective attention deficit disorder. You might say we're more than a little overstimulated.

There's a scene from a few summers ago I still can't get out of my head. I was standing in line to board a plane in Kansas City surrounded by about 15 people, all of whom were engaged in some sort of über-intimate communion with their phones. No one was looking at or talking to anyone else; they were staring intensely into their phones as if they were hooked up to some sort of life-giving IV line. The whole scene reminded me of one of those old 1960s-era horror movies where all the people are connected to the protoplasmic pod from another planet via the same subcutaneous, milky-looking umbilical tube, through which their brains are being slowly sucked out—resulting in the inured, glassy-eyed, blank stare of something not human, something from another world. It was *Invasion of the Body Snatchers* played out in real life. There was something simultaneously surreal and disturbing about that moment.

Yes, we've been assimilated and cloned without feeling a thing. Big Brother now has our brain on network, with unlimited data and access to boot.

Texting, as opposed to "talking" or "writing," has become our go-to mode of communication, which, as we've all discovered, can be a highly suspect method of interaction, fraught with confusion and misunderstanding. It's like we've devolved to the level of cavemen, drawing pictures on the wall to tell our story, speaking in symbols, hoping others can fill in the blanks to make up the rest of the narrative. Case in point, some major corporations have resorted to holding "communication" classes for new employees specifically aimed at training them in the once commonplace practice of face-to-face conversation! Apparently, all those hours we've spent hooked up to video games and iPhones haven't done much to improve our relational skills. All this technology, all these devices vying for our attention may have changed things for the worse because they ultimately crowd out meaningful dialogue with one another. The end result: isolation.

Can we get off the infotainment merry-go-round long enough to take a breath? We seem to excel at wandering from one distraction to the next, rarely stopping to assess whether or not we are headed in the right direction—or in any direction at all for that matter. We might be well-served to periodically stop and take a personal inventory aimed at critically evaluating the course of our lives.

Perhaps the area that has suffered most is our spiritual life. We're pretty good at entertaining ourselves and keeping ourselves busy with life in general, but what's going on inside of us? Maybe we're afraid to look very closely at ourselves because the lack of real depth and substance at the core of all our activities would be too shocking to even contemplate, so we simply keep on moving, oblivious to the consequences of an unexamined life.

Deep down, people in our culture are starving for meaning and significance. In fact, I'm convinced that the majority of the mass shootings (excluding those attributed to terror groups) we now see occurring so frequently are about nothing so much as getting noticed. People feel insignificant and powerless, so they do something, anything, to be noticed, to have their afternoon of fame—or infamy, as it always ends up being.

Eventually we have to deal with the interior life. If we're not willing to go there ourselves, some life event or crisis will eventually force us there, bringing us to a point where we have to stop and consider what we are doing and why we are doing it. That leads to the consideration of motive and belief.

Why do I feel the way I do, and can I, without violating my conscience, continue to act the way I'm acting and to believe what I'm believing? We have to make time to question our motives and examine what premises we are basing our lives upon.

According to Jesus Christ, the issue lies within our hearts. He asserts that what escapes our mouth into the world outside us is a direct reflection of our heart condition. According to Him, this simple fact prevails: What is on the inside of us will eventually come out of us. Be it good or bad, it will come to the surface. In Luke 6:45, Jesus defines the inside-outside dynamic for us:

> "The good man out of the good treasure of his heart brings forth what is good; and the evil man out of the evil treasure brings forth what is evil; for his mouth speaks from that which fills his heart."

But is it really that simple, that black and white? Are we in one camp or the other, with no in-between? Is God going to judge us based solely on what camp we are a member of, or will He weigh our good and bad deeds in the balance, assigning us either a passing or failing grade based upon a preponderance of evidence favoring one status or the other?

To be fair, the issue here is not only our behavior; it is our "standing" before a holy God, for God's holiness is defined by perfection—a foreign state of existence to all of us. We bristle at being held up to such an exalted standard, but after all, we certainly wouldn't choose to swear allegiance to a god who is flawed in any way, would we? All facets of His character must be beyond reproach. His holiness—far from being merely an abstract, religious expression—is what makes Him worthy of our love and trust.

A commonly held misconception—one that has only been reinforced by many religions—is that God's holiness renders

Him unapproachable. However, when you read the Bible, you will encounter a God who is intimately involved with His creation. If we go missing in action, He comes looking for us. If we are in distress, He is there. The Psalms, all 150 of them, are replete with accounts of people who alternately felt close to and/or far from God at a given point in their lives. These "songs" cover the entire spectrum of human experience from indescribable joy to abject tragedy. They remind us that God is still present in the midst of whatever circumstances in which we find ourselves.

Difficult circumstances, however, often create obstacles capable of breaking down our communication with our Creator. Real tragedy or suffering often arouses anger at our situation, and we are prone to blame God instead of doing the hard work of wrestling with the inevitable emotional turmoil and struggle.

We have this desperate need to find a scapegoat, but if we insist on being both judge and jury, we are leaving God out of the picture, making judgments only He is qualified to render. We see this emotional tug-of-war played out in many of the aforementioned Psalms, which so often depict this entire emotional cycle beginning with adversity, then indignation (at the adversity), then anger, then acceptance of circumstances, and then ending with (for the most part) trust in God to direct the outcome of those situations. Yes, people have even been angry at and disappointed with God and have lived to tell about it.

So, God is trying to reach out to us. He wants to reveal Himself to us. But—what's our interest level? Relationships involve give-and-take, and our relationship with God is no different from any other relationship we are part of: We have to invest time and effort into it if we expect it to satisfy. More than once, Jesus said this: "He who has ears to hear, let him hear." Obviously, all of us have ears. Some of us are using them to listen and to look for God. Some of us just have ears.

If we are listening, most of us will eventually realize God has unique qualities at His disposal. Though our capacity to love is derived from being created in His image (see Genesis 1:26), and human love is certainly capable of "mirroring" God's love, it is also limited in part by our propensity for self-interest and self-sustenance. God's love is "agape" love, that which is dedicated to the flourishing and flowering of His creation, of which we, believe it or not, are the foremost examples. All of creation, the populating of the earth with vegetation and animals, the creation of man and woman—all of it was an intentional act of love on God's part.

Before Adam and Eve sinned, they enjoyed the purity of this mutually loving relationship with God in the Garden of Eden and related to Him unencumbered by any guilt or self-consciousness. They were able to relate to God without any static disrupting the communication lines; that is, they understood Him perfectly and were willing to accept His leadership and guidance. But once they sinned, their nature was corrupted, and both of them began to feel shame, self-consciousness, and fear. In fact, their first act upon disobeying God was to hide from Him! The relationship developed a deep fissure, a brokenness which, unfortunately, we, their descendants, inherited. What sin has left us with is this tendency toward control and self-determination, but at what cost?

In a sense, God then had a problem to solve. He could have simply exterminated His creation for disobeying his directions, opting out of the whole arrangement. After all, He is God and doesn't need us to exist, so why would He spare Noah and his sons through the Flood and prolong the agony of humankind's destitute brokenness (see Genesis, chapter 6)?

Perhaps God's own character, His "holiness," would not allow Him to simply turn completely away from us. He cannot deny Himself, can He? And since God is love, and love as we understand it must have an object of affection to be love, then God must be true to His own character. He cannot abandon His creation. Hence, He spared Noah, a "righteous" man (Genesis 6:9) and his family.

I submit to you, then, the idea that holiness is not simply the absence of evil, but, moreover, it is the presence of love, which has far-reaching implications for us—the object of that love.

2
MERCY FINDS US

MOST OF US have learned what love is over time and trial. As we accumulate experiences, we discover that it encompasses many qualities beyond unbridled passion, such as forgiveness, mercy, kindness, affection, and truthfulness. Mercy, in particular, seems to be one of the highest, most magnanimous qualities, for mercy attaches value to that which does not deserve value. Couched in the middle of the book of James, in the second chapter, the thirteenth verse, is a statement that may be the penultimate expression of this quality:

> For judgment will be merciless to one who has shown no mercy; **mercy triumphs over judgment.** (James 2:13)

This verse follows an earlier lesson in the chapter regarding how to treat people—especially the poor—impartially and without showing favor, but it has a much more far-reaching application. Mercy is not merely a good thing; it is *triumphant*, the highest expression of love. It is in one sense the most resounding message found in the Bible. It is this degree of love that is embodied in the person of Jesus Christ.

Despite His overtures of mercy, we are still prone to believe that God's sole purpose is to impose upon us a set of rules by which He can control us, but in reality, He is doing exactly the opposite. He frees us from the tyranny of religion, of "rule-keeping," by extending mercy to us in the form of acceptance and forgiveness in the person of Jesus Christ. He knows we are not capable of appreciating the benefits of the "rules" unless we first understand that He loves us *even when we fail to keep the rules.* Understanding mercy, then, as the repairing and restoring of our relationship to our Creator will help us to understand the differences between religion and God's gift of mercy.

Author Timothy Keller distinguishes between the two this way: "Religion says, 'I obey; therefore I'm accepted.' The Gospel (of Jesus Christ) says, 'I'm *accepted*, therefore, I obey.'"[1] This is the difference between obeying out of obligation or guilt or, conversely, experiencing God's forgiveness through a conscious choice you make; it is the difference between obeying to avoid punishment or wanting to do it out of gratitude for a gift one has received.

To experience God's acceptance, we must approach Him and ask Him to fix our brokenness (that is the "gift" He is offering), and then God will aid us in understanding that the rules are beneficial to us, for any "rules" made by our Designer are made by one who understands the necessary degree of structure required for His creation to thrive to its fullest measure.

God's mercy makes it possible for us to take the first step toward Him, toward understanding the depth of His love for us. We need to adopt the attitude of the woman in Mark 5:28 who believed that all she had to do was touch the hem of Jesus's cloak and she would be healed of a hemorrhage that had plagued her for 12 years. She fought her way through the crowd to get to Him, and in Mark 5:34, Jesus acknowledged that He was aware of her presence and her need:

> "Daughter, your faith has made you well; go in peace and be healed of your affliction."

Once you begin moving toward God, He will continue to draw you to Jesus Christ. You may encounter some obstacles along the way, but do not be distracted or deterred from reaching Jesus.

Where should you start? Finding a Bible-believing church (or at least a group of believers who meet together on a regular basis) is paramount to making your journey a success. If that route is not immediately available, then find a person who has a relationship with Jesus Christ and ask them to be your guide. If you don't know anyone who knows Christ, then ask God to bring that person to you. He will.

How exactly will all of this happen for you? Only God knows the prescribed circumstances by which you will encounter Him, but be assured that He is *actively* looking for you. Your part is to keep moving toward Jesus Christ, and He will do the rest. His greatest desire is to heal the relationship that has been broken, to restore your ability to communicate with Him.

We were not meant to live apart from God, to "hide" from Him. He will go to great lengths to reach you. The best example of this quality is found in the Gospel of Luke in the New Testament. In chapter 15, Jesus tells three stories, or "parables," that reveal how He truly feels about us.

He compares our relationship with Him to that of a shepherd who has lost a sheep and leaves his post to look for that one lost sheep. Think of a time when you couldn't find your missing son or daughter, and the panic that set in, and you will approximate the urgency God feels toward us when we are living life apart from Him, separated from Him, pursuing our own agenda exclusively.

When the shepherd finds the sheep, it is the source of a deep, resounding joy far more satisfying to him than anything else. Time to throw a party! He (Jesus) also talks about losing money, which all of us have done, sweeping the house to find it—and then the immense relief that comes when you finally discover it. Then there is the joy of telling your friends about it so they can rejoice with you.

Finally, He recounts the story of a devoted father whose son did not want to live under his father's legacy but instead wanted to go out into the world to forge his own destiny. Unfortunately, he quickly squandered the inheritance money his father had given him and fell on hard times, becoming desperate for help. He couldn't even feed himself.

With no other options left, he returned to his boyhood home, hoping his father might let him work there as a hired hand. Can you imagine the shame and embarrassment he felt? He was probably expecting an "I told you so" speech, but his father would have none of that, though, and instead threw him a magnificent party to celebrate his return! No expense was spared. Only the best for his *prodigal* son. Of course, these examples are only word pictures of God's love. The real thing is amazing to behold, especially when you see it take hold of a person's heart—or better yet, your own heart.

Is this picture of God's personality beginning to take shape for you? Far from being a mere laboratory curiosity He occasionally pokes and prods, in God's eyes we represent something worth looking far and wide for because, to Him, we are as *buried treasure*. He places immense value upon us. Here in these parables, Jesus communicates the depth and breadth of His love for us, which is manifested in His pursuit of us. Each of us is worth far more than any momentary obligation or activity. We are His one overriding concern, and the passion exhibited by God in pursuing us is beyond comparison. He is calling out to us, trying to locate us, just as He called out to Adam and Eve after they hid from God because of their sin:

> Then the Lord God called to the man, and said to him, "Where are you?" (Genesis 3:9)

Like the two of them, we tend to go missing-in-action, a condition due either to the myriad distractions the world offers—or whatever sin in which we choose to indulge. We must strain valiantly against both of these saboteurs if we are to avoid falling headlong into the error of Adam and Eve, whose shame compelled them to hide from the Lord, their God. Shame is a soul-destroying monster because it uses our own pride against us. We don't want to be embarrassed, so we would rather avoid anyone we think might find our behavior substandard, God included. The problem is that the fear of embarrassment isolates us from the only One who can help us overcome the very cause of our shame!

Thus, we must never give up on ourselves and give in to a sin because we are tired of fighting its allure. If we quit resisting temptation, then the vicious cycle of shame kicks in and we are in grave spiritual danger. Just as Adam and Eve ran from God, we end up hiding from God and those who care the most about us. Indeed, this problem can manifest itself in any of our personal relationships. If someone is "hiding" from you, they may very well be dealing with shame in some form.

If we are to avoid this pitfall, we must acknowledge the depth and breadth of God's love and forgiveness. Keep confessing, keep humbling yourself before God. Is it embarrassing to continue struggling with the same issue time after time? Yes, but *use the embarrassment* as fuel for the battle. Turn your anger against the sin because it is trying to destroy your soul and rob you of your relationships with God and those you care about! Remember this: No matter what you have done, no matter how many times you have done it, Christ stands ready to forgive if you are willing to humble yourself before Him.

If you have not yet encountered Jesus Christ, yet the desire is present in you, then God will help you. He is seeking us, trying to bring us out of hiding. But there is another aspect to this dance: *We* can also initiate the restoring of the relationship by returning home willingly as the prodigal son did. We can certainly leave God to chase us alone, but we can also accelerate the reunification process by turning toward Him.

The truth is: Without God, we are destitute and broken, no matter what our worldly status or achievements may say to others about our natural abilities. Without Him we are living in poverty because we were created to live not only in the natural but also in the supernatural realm, our relationship with Jesus Christ being the core relationship we were created to enjoy and thrive within.

To summarize, whatever joy and contentment you may have discovered without God is a pale imitation of what He intends for you to experience. It may be a good and comfortable state you find yourself in, but sometimes the *merely good* is the worst enemy of the *great*.

We have discussed God's agape love for us, but to what extent is He interested in how we live our lives day-to-day? We need Him to give us understanding as to what He does and doesn't want for us. We are not on the point system, nor are we even being graded on the "curve." In fact, our standing before God does not depend upon our merit at all:

> He saved us, **not on the basis of deeds which we have done** in righteousness, but **according to His mercy**, by the washing of regeneration and renewing by the Holy Spirit. (Titus 3:5)

In other words, we cannot "work" our way to heaven, nor will God accept us on the basis of how many "good" deeds we do. If you chafe at that notion, then consider the implications of being judged on your performance alone. How would you ever know if you had done enough to appease God? Exactly how many "points" would one have to earn or accumulate to make it into heaven?

We would be left dangling in the wind, never knowing if we had done enough to make the grade. That would be far more cruel than the truth, which is that God understands our imperfection; it's not a deal-breaker, it does not negate His love for us, and, in fact, He has acted on our behalf to solve the problem for us.

He states that only *His* mercy saves us. The one "deed" or performance that matters to God has already taken place: the crucifixion of Jesus Christ. What God allowed to happen to His Son on the cross was an intentional sacrifice, a deliberate act of love staged at an actual moment in this time-space continuum we call history. This moment of sacrifice was God's way of solving our sin problem and restoring our broken relationship with Him.

Instead of each of us suffering death for our sinfulness, Christ died in our place, as our substitute, taking upon Himself the shame of sin and the wrath of God against sin. Why this plan? Because all of humankind, past, present, and future, would be irreparably separated from God without His own supernatural intervention on our behalf.

God has addressed our inside issue, our heart problem. If we will accept the gift of forgiveness Christ purchased for us by His substitutionary death, we won't be left to look for meaning in our electronic devices, drugs, social media, or the variety of other diversions and temporarily satisfying, seductive pleasures the world has to offer. What He has provided is far more lasting and fulfilling: the unrivaled fullness of a living, active, life-sustaining relationship with

Him.

It's the one essential thing worth embracing in this life.

3
KNOWING GOD

LET'S GET HYPOTHETICAL for a minute. If necessary, suspend your disbelief in the concept of "God" for a moment, and allow your mind to navigate among some of the potential big questions surrounding this subject. Is there a god, and if there is, can we know Him? If God is good, why does He allow so much evil in the world? How can you have faith in a god you can't see?

Those are all valid questions, subjects many people dismiss outright or don't want to think about—or at least would rather delay thinking about until they find themselves in a situation that requires their consideration, such as impending death. After all, these are such immense questions, and who can state with any degree of certainty what the answers should be? Can't we just ignore God and live our lives doing whatever we wish? Isn't God merely an invention of the collective human psyche designed to pacify or comfort us on some superficial level, with religion being the "opiate of the masses" as German philosopher Karl Marx termed it?

So many questions, and has anyone answered them? Humankind has been wrestling with finding and then understanding God for centuries, and we see that struggle reflected in arts and literature through time.

One such example is Leo Tolstoy's late-nineteenth century novella, *The Death of Ivan Ilyich*, in which we meet a man who, through his own choices, has isolated himself from anyone who might possibly care about him.[2] Ivan Ilyich is an upward-striving middle class bureaucrat working in the Russian government. He is obsessed with his social standing and what other people think of him.

When a seemingly innocuous injury to his side does not heal properly and renders him bedridden, he finds himself approaching life's end without a single soul he can claim as a genuine friend. In fact, his own wife and daughter are so emotionally distant he feels they have abandoned him and left him to the ravages of his infirmity.

Ivan's bereft condition is salved only by his household servant, Gerasim, whose compassionate caretaking of Ivan begins to awaken something in him, forcing Ivan to examine how he has lived his life. Only then does he come to the realization that he has lived only for himself, that he has not loved as he should have, and, most significantly, that he is, at the core of his being, *empty*. His life has been a wholly vacuous endeavor.

Gerasim cares for Ivan in his deteriorating condition, not because he deserves it, but because *that is who Gerasim is*, and Ivan is deeply affected by his servant's unsolicited compassion. He begins to contemplate what place God (and people) should have had in his barren existence. After a bedside visit from his quietly grieving schoolboy son, he realizes his life does not have to end in bitter regret. He is finally able to ask for forgiveness in his final hours. It's a moving and relevant story, especially if we can muster the courage to examine our own life through Tolstoy's vantage point.

We share many traits with Ivan Ilyich, one in particular that betrays our humanness: We all want to feel *significant*. We instinctively want to be part of something bigger than ourselves. On some level, we want our lives to matter to someone other than ourselves. Consider the possibility that we do, in fact, matter to someone greater than ourselves, namely God. Suppose He created us for the purpose of loving us, for the purpose of guiding us and infusing our lives with meaning and purpose. If we are to believe John 17:3, He created us to be in *relationship* with Him:

> "And this is eternal life that they may **know** You, the only true God, and Jesus Christ whom You have sent." (John 17:3)

That word "know" has some different shades of depth to it, doesn't it? I mean it's one thing to know *about* someone, but it's completely different to actually *know* that person. We all know something about, for example, the actor Tom Hanks, but very few of us know him personally and have a living, active relationship with him. Big, big difference.

So, God has much more in mind for us than merely providing some fire insurance for the future. The God who presents Himself in the Bible is a God of *relationship*, in addition to being transcendent, all-powerful, and all the many other ways in which He is different from us. Primarily though, He, as God, *knows* His creation on an individual level and wants *to be known* by His creation on the most intimate level possible. That doesn't sound very "religious," does it?

I truly believe God has given us some very specific means by which we can maintain our relationship with Him. In fact, He wants us so close that we would draw our very sustenance for living from Him. In John 15:4-5, He adjures us to be even more than that—not merely close, but *attached* to Him:

> "Abide in Me, and I in you. As the branch cannot bear fruit of itself unless it abides in the vine, so neither can you unless you abide in Me. I am the vine, you are the branches; he who abides in Me and I in him, he bears much fruit, for apart from Me you can do nothing."

That's a pretty dramatic word picture. God wants us closer-than-close. He sees us as an extension of Himself, a branch of His life-giving vine, which is only possible on the real-world level if we take steps to cultivate and nourish our relationship with Him. Take note that this is a conditional statement, in the sense that Jesus ends it by saying: *"for apart from Me, you can do nothing."* In other words, we must remain connected to Him (the vine) if we are to function as we are intended to function. We all know that a vine ultimately withers and dies if it is severed from the main branch, so the connection must be maintained at all costs.

So, how do we connect *with* God in the real world? I believe we can come to God as is because He rewards people who seek Him (Hebrews 11:6). Since you must spend time with someone to get to know them, what follows is a simple pattern for spending time with God and getting to know Him—highly recommended for those curious about or interested in either inaugurating or maintaining a relationship with Him. Every day, Monday through Friday, I try to spend some time listening to God and, in turn, letting Him know what's on my mind.

I usually begin with a short prayer asking God to reveal Himself to me, and then begin with…

I. Reading the Bible (5 to 10 minutes)

There are several books of the Bible that are good starting points. I would suggest exploring any of the following:

A. The Gospel of John (New Testament): Read a chapter every day. It's an excellent introduction to the person of Jesus Christ, and it offers substantial detail about our relationship with Him.

B. The Psalms (Old Testament): There are 150 psalms, so if you read five of them every day, you can make it through all 150 in a month. For example, on Day 1 you would read Psalms 1, 31, 61, 91, and 121. On Day 2, read

Psalms 2, 32, 62, 92, and 122, and so on and so on. Don't worry if you can't make it through all five every day. The Psalms are unique in that they cover the entire spectrum of the human experience. Every emotional state, from utter despair to exultant joy, can be found in its pages.

C. Genesis (Old Testament): It contains numerous historical accounts that illuminate God's character and how He communicates with those who believe in Him.

D. Proverbs (Old Testament): In this, the most practical of all biblical texts, resides a treasure of wisdom and instruction for living life successfully. There are 31 Proverbs, so you could read one each day of the month.

Reading the Bible is like looking in a mirror; it tells us the truth about God and the truth about ourselves, and truth changes us. It has a hidden benefit that distinguishes it from any other book: Because it is inspired by God, it has the supernatural power to change our hearts, to change us from the inside out. Romans 10:17 says this:

So faith comes from hearing, and hearing by the word of Christ.

The Bible is His primary method of speaking to us, and if we are to hear Him, we need to spend time reading it.

You may also choose to use one of the many available devotional guides, which you can find at almost any bookstore, Christian or otherwise. *Our Daily Bread* is a very popular one that many churches make available to people for free. Typically these publications contain a selection for every day of the year, and they are an excellent tool for introducing yourself to the Bible, especially if you are a new believer.

II. Memorizing Scripture (2 to 3 minutes)

As I read the Bible, I often come across a verse or group of verses that I find inspirational. I may spend two or three minutes trying to memorize that verse. I use a method derived from the *Topical Memory System*, published by NavPress.[3] First, I assign a topic to the verse, such as "Serving God," then I quote the verse reference, such as Mark 10:45. Then, I recite the verse, breaking it up into sections depending on the length. You must find your own rhythm, but here is how I would divide this verse for memorization:

1. For even the Son of Man did not come to be served,
2. But to serve,
3. And to give His life
4. A ransom for many.

Then I conclude by reciting the reference again: Mark 10:45. It's very helpful to have a stack of note cards to write verses down on, or you may be able to record and save them on your phone. Memorizing and then meeting together with a friend or a small group to discuss the verses is a great way to get to know God and each other.

III. Prayer (5-10 minutes)

I like to use the A-C-T-S prayer model during my time with the Lord. The letters in the acrostic represent these ideas:

A—Adoration

This is a time where we praise God for His goodness, His love and the other qualities that we draw inspiration from. Read the Psalms, and discover the joy of praising God. These writings are a great source to draw from when it comes to describing God and all His attributes. Check out the book of Isaiah, chapters 43 through 53, which also describe the greatness and uniqueness of God.

C—Confession

This is such an important part of prayer that it has been described as "spiritual breathing." As I confess my sin, I exhale, and then I inhale as I accept God's forgiveness. 1 John 1:9 says,

> If we confess our sins, He is faithful and righteous to forgive us our sins and to cleanse us from all unrighteousness.

God's forgiveness is not restricted by your weakness or struggles; it is always there if you keep confessing. He does not turn His back on or give up on us. If you are struggling with a particular issue, it may help to have an accountability partner, someone you can share your confession with, a trustworthy Christian friend who will pray for you and support you.

T—Thanksgiving

This is the part we often forget, but it's an incredibly important attitude we need to cultivate. We need to thank God for the good as well as the bad moments that happen because both extremes are part of who we are and how God shapes our character. Romans 8:28 says,

> And we know that God causes all things to work together for good to those who love God, to those who are called according to His purpose.

While we may not enjoy some of our experiences, they are all worthy of a thankful attitude.

S—Supplication

This is where we ask God for specifics, praying for individuals in our lives and bringing all our concerns before the throne of God. Sometimes the answer is "yes," sometimes it's "no," and very often, it is "wait," but whatever the outcome, we need to think less about the results of our prayers and more about the joy of cultivating our relationship with the Lord. One word of caution: God is not a vending machine; you put in your money and out comes exactly what you want. Think of it more as a conversation, with God revealing His will to you step by step.

I truly believe God would rather have 10 to 15 good minutes with us every day as opposed to one fantastic hour a week. If we truly want to know God and be used by Him, our faith cannot be a one-day-a-week event. We need to live and breathe it every day.

Don't neglect the most important relationship in your life.

4
THE QUESTION OF GOOD AND EVIL

WHEN WE LOOK at the state of the world, it's not always easy to conceive of a god whose basic nature is to love his creation and whose character would be deemed "good." We ask ourselves the question, "If God is good, then why does He allow so much evil in this world?" That seems like a paradox, but not if you consider God's nature and personality.

The Bible says, "...God **is** love" (1 John 4:8), but love is not love unless it allows both the one who loves and the object of that love the freedom to accept or reject it. In other words, if one is forced to love another out of fear or manipulation, that is not love; that is compulsion or coercion. Both parties must be able to *freely* exercise their will in the giving and receiving of affection. Hence, the Creator of the universe gives His love to us freely, unconditionally, but God, being true to His nature, will not force us to love Him in return. He gives us the freedom to respond to that love—or to reject it.

Bottom line: God will not violate our free will. We are not puppets; we are creatures who make choices. Those choices are sometimes good and aligned with God's will, thus promoting the purposes of God and the welfare of others, but they can also be evil and destructive to others and to us as well. How we use our freedom is up to us, but to ensure our freedom is preserved, God must, by necessity of love, allow our choices to play out in real life. Therefore, He permits evil to coexist alongside good. Fortunately, He has solved our biggest challenge in making good choices—the very problem that creates evil (our sinful, selfish nature)—by giving us the opportunity to *escape* the power of sin.

Now we're getting down to the nitty-gritty, down to the level where we live and play. First, let me get real for a second about the reality of sin. What I'm about to say is in no way meant to condemn or judge anyone. For me personally, the awareness of sin was there even before I believed in Christ, but it was not the only significant motivating factor in my pursuit of God; it was also triggered by the emptiness and lack of significance I felt. In fact, not until Christ came into my life did I fully begin to understand the destructive power sin could exert over my life.

Put simply, sin is a spiritual force that manifests itself in any thought (yes, we are responsible for what traffics through our waking mind) or behavior that is contrary or opposed to God's truth.

Because we are accountable to God, we need to first learn His perspective on sin and then understand why we need to be saved from it.

That said, sin is not some quaint religious word or outdated expression that no longer has any relevance in the twenty-first century. Unfortunately, it's a fact of life, and we see the outward expression of it every day in our lives and the lives of others. As children, we learn the art of being selfish, fighting with our siblings for control, and then developing sinful patterns that often extend into our teenage and early adult years. If you are (or ever have been) married, then you have an intimate understanding of how selfish and self-centered we are all capable of being. Am I right?

For that matter, at some point in all your long-term relationships—be they romantic, family, or friendship—you have no doubt had to deal with your own or someone else's self-centeredness and bad behavior. God calls this selfish behavior "sin." I think I'm speaking pretty plainly here; you don't need a doctorate in psychology or theology to understand that none of us is perfect. In fact, one of the translations of the word "sin" in the Bible literally means, "to miss the mark"—a result all of us are familiar with on an almost-everyday basis.

God, however, *is perfect,* He *is holy,* and He *is offended* by our sin. In Romans 3:23, the Apostle Paul states:

> "For all have sinned and fall short of the **glory** of God."

In Isaiah 59:2a, the Prophet Isaiah says:

> "But your iniquities [sins] have made a **separation** between you and your God."

In fact, God has declared that the penalty for our sin is death—both spiritual and physical.

Romans 6:23 reads:

> For the wages of sin is death....

In other words, there is a price to be paid for sin, and that price is death.

However, there is more to Romans 6:23. The verse ends with this rejoinder:

> ...but the **free gift** of God is eternal life in Christ Jesus our Lord.

The facts are harsh, but the solution to our dilemma is a glorious one. God has provided an escape clause, a way out of death!

The *cost* of sin was paid for by Jesus. Throughout the Old and New Testaments in the Bible, God requires the "shedding of blood" as payment (or "atonement") for our sin (see

Hebrews 9:22). This is why Jesus had to shed His blood on the cross. He paid our debt, once and for all, to God. His shed blood was the currency by which our forgiveness was purchased. When Jesus died on the cross, he uttered this expression: "It is finished," a literal translation of the Greek word, *"tetelestai"* (John 19:28).[4]

This word has several shades of meaning, such as to bring to completion, to fulfill, to accomplish, or to finish. Some biblical scholars believe it was used in the marketplace at that time to indicate that a debt had been paid in full, or satisfied. In the context of Jesus's death, then, we can readily understand why He uttered this expression. He was testifying of the finality of His work on earth.

Each one of us should be tasting death for our sin, but God provided Christ as a substitute: a perfect, unblemished lamb put to death as satisfaction for our debt. This explains John the Baptist's proclamation in John 1:29 as Jesus approached him: "Behold, the Lamb of God who takes away the sin of the world!"

Jesus purchased our forgiveness through this single, solitary act that occurred in Jerusalem some 2,000 years ago.

What Jesus has purchased for us—the gift of eternal life (spoken of in Romans 6:23)—is not yours until you reach out and take hold of it, which is where faith enters the picture. God requires that we only believe in Jesus's sacrificial death to receive this gift. What constitutes belief? That is between you and God.

For me, it happened gradually over the course of maybe 18 months, the last six of which were spent investigating the Bible and going to church. Finally, I reached a point where I was convinced enough to tell God that I wanted to be with Him. What happened next I cover elsewhere in this book, but let's say that just as Jesus was resurrected from the grave and now lives on as Lord over all creation, I, too, experienced a "resurrection."

God doesn't save you and then leave you to manage as best you can; He transforms you into a new person (2 Corinthians 5:17) and empowers you to live a life glorifying to God. More about that later.

So, for some of us, our spiritual awakening may come along the lines of sin-awareness, but it can also begin as we realize there is someone greater than ourselves who wants to inject meaning and purpose into our lives. When we realize that Jesus Christ is the answer, not only to our sin problem but also to our need for love, then we are ready to respond to His offer of forgiveness.

Our response, be it acceptance or rejection, was embodied in history by the two criminals who were crucified together with Jesus. One man sarcastically implored Jesus to save Himself since He was the Christ (Luke 23:39), while the other beseeched Jesus to "remember me when You come in your kingdom" (Luke 23:42). One man responded in sarcasm, the other in humility. Their responses are in one sense a microcosm of all humanity: We possess either a heart that is skeptical or one that is willing to risk trusting God. The skeptical man did not realize that Jesus possessed that which he desperately needed. He only resented his own misery.

Do not fall through that same trap door and miss out on what God has for you.

God loves us and desires to draw us into an intimate relationship as we repent and experience His forgiveness through Christ, but if we resist, He will not—in a sense, He *cannot*—force us into that relationship because that would contradict His very nature. As stated earlier, He will not force us to do good or evil or to choose Him over our sin. Even from the beginning, in the Garden of Eden, God permitted Adam and Eve to choose for themselves. Many people reduce the couple's choice to merely good versus evil, but on a deeper level, it was also a choice to trust, or not trust, their Creator for life's provision.

Will evil people and evil actions eventually receive their just punishment? Yes, but God has reserved for Himself the right to pronounce the day and time of that final judgment. Until then, life goes on, and we must live out our lives in the presence of both good and evil. Given then this equation, it is crucial we understand the key issue we need to address in spite of evil. Jesus highlights it for us in Luke 13:1-5:

> Now on the same occasion there were some present who reported to Him about the Galileans whose blood Pilate had mixed with their sacrifices. And Jesus said to them, "Do you suppose that these Galileans were greater sinners than all other Galileans because they suffered this fate? I tell you, no, but **unless you repent**, you will all likewise perish. Or do you suppose that those eighteen on whom the tower in Siloam fell and killed them were worse culprits than all the men who live in Jerusalem? I tell you, no, but **unless you repent**, you will all likewise perish."

What is Jesus getting at here? Is He saying the tower of Siloam (verse 4) fell on these people because they were really bad and deserved this sorry fate more than the next person? Is He giving us an ultimatum? No, but He is explaining the two possible outcomes of the most critical decision a human being can ever make. He is telling us that, hey, guess what, stuff happens, sometimes evil stuff, and unless you want to be just another faceless victim of one of life's many tragedies (like the people in Siloam) then you must *repent*.

Why repent? Repentance means to change direction, to turn away from what you are doing now and to turn toward the Lord Jesus. It is not optional; it is a requirement for redemption. Repentance is the door every single human being must walk through to enter into a *relationship* with the Lord. When we turn to Christ, we cease being a victim of life or death, and we begin to really live for the first time.

Second Peter 3:9 puts it most profoundly:

> The Lord is not slow about His promise, as some count slowness, but is patient toward you, **not wishing for any to perish** but for all to come to repentance.

The world at large, especially the politically correct contingent, would have you believe that all religions lead to the same place, to the same god. However, Jesus Christ does not give you the option of choosing a "religion" as your path to knowing God. In fact, He claims that the only way to know God is not via religion but through *Himself* (John 14:6). This is radical because He is making the case **against** *religion*, and **for** *relationship* with the one true God.

Religion is us jumping through the hoops we believe God has set up for us, trying to keep the rules well enough to merit His approval, trying to be "good" enough to make the grade. True, accurate, spiritual self-appraisal is me realizing that I am sinful and *separated* (the relationship is broken) from God and in need of something greater than myself to bridge the gap—the equivalent of a mediator who can reconcile me to God. Jesus makes this crystal clear in the Gospels, and there are numerous passages in the balance of the New Testament that support this assertion. Jesus, in one sense, is our "advocate," the only one who is qualified to litigate our case before God the Father:

> For there is **one God**, and **one mediator** also between God and men, the man Christ Jesus, who gave himself as ransom for all. (1 Timothy 2:5-6a)

One God. **One** mediator. This singular solution has staggering implications for us then when we examine the myriad of ways in which we try to relate to God and earn His approval. If what Jesus said is true, then practicing religion will not please God. Neither can you please Him by being a "good" person who does more good than bad (keeping score). Nor can you get there by taking the generic approach, incorporating a little bit of everything into a user-friendly sort of "supermarket" spirituality, combining what you like about various religions or lifestyles into your own homemade spirituality. Being a follower of the prophet Muhammad (Islam), Joseph Smith (Mormonism), or Mahatma Gandhi, or practicing Buddhism or transcendental meditation, will not usher you into God's presence or earn His favor.

You can only arrive there by going through *one door*: Jesus Christ. Hebrews 9:22 says,

> ...without shedding of blood there is no forgiveness.

Christ shed His blood for **you**. He *alone* purchased your salvation through this act. He gave His life as a ransom (Mark 10:45) in exchange for yours. This is the distinctive claim that separates Him from all forms of religion. When Jesus said, "*I am the way, and the truth, and the life; no one comes to the Father but through Me*" (John 14:6), He was declaring Himself—**not religion or doing good deeds**—to be the **sole** agent of reconciliation between God and humankind.

If we do not turn toward Jesus at some point in our lives to acknowledge God's action on our behalf, then, in effect, we have made the decision *not* to repent. By either our aggressive disbelief or passive indifference, we have exercised our option to tell God "no." No, I don't want your offer of forgiveness and, no, I don't want a relationship with you. God, in His Fatherly love, will honor your choice, and He will also let you experience the consequences of your decision.

Before you make that decision, consider this one unalterable fact: you only have this lifetime to decide, and once you pass out of this physical life into death, the deal is done, and it becomes an <u>irrevocable</u> decision (Hebrews 9:27).

There are no second chances, no do-overs, no coming back (reincarnation) as someone else. There is only judgment and, as a result, either the joy of eternal **union** (John 5:24) with God or the pain of eternal **separation** (2 Thessalonians 1:9) from Him. This isn't tee ball, where every kid gets a medal or trophy simply for showing up. This "game" of life is for real, and it's the ultimate high-stakes game, one being waged for people's lives, for *your life*, in fact. In the end, only one team wins. The alternative? A pastor friend of mine once described it in terms similar to this: *If the desire of our heart is to keep God at arm's length, then He will grant us that desire.*

Your move.

5
THE NATURE OF FAITH

> Then he believed in the Lord; and He reckoned it to him as righteousness. (Genesis 15:6)
>
> Not that we are adequate in ourselves to consider anything as coming from ourselves, but our adequacy is from God. (2 Corinthians 3:5)

OUR FAITH MUST begin somehow, somewhere; it must originate from a source greater than ourselves—the object of our faith. We can't muster it or grind it up from inside of us. You cannot get something *supernatural* from what is natural (us). Faith is a two-party system consisting of a benefactor, the object of our faith, and a beneficiary, the receiver of all the benefactor has to offer in reward for faith. So, by definition, it requires the supernatural assistance and partnership of a loving, generous supreme being. It is far more than an attitude or idea; it is, above all else, a gift.

People have debated and pontificated forever on the subject of faith, but it's not a topic that lends itself to being easily defined by universals, platitudes, or instructional books. It's more of an individual matter between you and God, and were we to conduct some man-on-the-street interviews and ask people to define what faith is, the variety of perspectives offered would be astonishing. It is difficult to describe in words a concept that belongs to the "spirit" world, the unseen world. What transpires between God and us when we get on our knees to seek Him is the very stuff of life. Will we believe? That is the question. Do we believe in God, and do we believe He will respond when we call upon Him?

We typically view faith as our idea, as something that

begins with us and exists for our benefit. However, the Bible clearly indicates that even faith is God's idea, not ours. What we can say with absolute surety is that faith originates with God:

> For by grace you have been saved through faith, and that not of yourselves, it is the **gift** of God; not as a result of works, that no one may boast. (Ephesians 2:8-9)

We cannot take credit for it; we can only receive it as a gift directly from His hand. Wait a minute, though, doesn't God evaluate us on the basis of how "big" our faith is, how many prayers are answered, and how long we spend in prayer each day? To be fair, there are a number of religions that are predicated on a prescribed regimen of prayer. Muslims practice "salat," which requires them to pray five times daily and is considered the second-most important of Islam's five pillars.[5] If my understanding is correct, Muslims view this as a way to establish contact with God through ritual prayer.

The God of the Bible, however, is not about ritualistic obligations. If you read the Old Testament, you will find that the Israelites, His people, repeatedly failed to keep the rituals, the Law, that God had instructed them to follow. They could not do it. They endlessly repeated the cycle of breaking God's laws, being disciplined by God for their failure, and then being restored by Him after the discipline was completed. They were incapable of following the instruction manual, which is why God inaugurated a "new" covenant, one that did not depend upon the ability of His people to conform outwardly to a list of rules and regulations.

This is described for us in Jeremiah 31:31-33:

> "Behold, days are coming," declares the Lord, "when I will make a new covenant with the house of Israel and with the house of Judah, **not like the covenant which I made with their fathers** in the day I took them by the hand to bring them out of the land of

> Egypt, My covenant which they broke, although I was a husband to them," declares the Lord. "But this is the covenant which I will make with the house of Israel after those days," declares the Lord, "**I will put My law within them and on their heart I will write it**; and I will be their God, and they shall be My people."

Reading this, we get the impression that God, at this point in history, had decided His people would never be able to make their inner beings conform to His outward requirements. A fundamental change in methodology was required. He decided change must occur from the inside out. In other words, He must change the heart of man by putting His Law "within them" and "writing it on their heart." In fact, He must give them a *new* heart. This idea would reach complete fruition when Jesus appeared on earth. He would inaugurate this new covenant by dying for the sins of the people. Later, He would describe the significance of His sacrifice to His disciples as they gathered together for the Last Supper:

> And in the same way He took the cup after they had eaten, saying, "This cup which is poured out for you is **the new covenant** in My blood." (Luke 22:20)

By His crucifixion and death—the shedding of His blood—He was removing the condemnation we had brought upon ourselves by our continual failure to keep God's laws:

> ...having canceled out the certificate of debt consisting of decrees against us, which was hostile to us; and He has taken it out of the way, having nailed it to the cross. (Colossians 2:14)

God creates a new heart within His people by changing them from the inside out. The way He chooses to do this is to impart His own life-giving spirit to them, to fill them with it. This is what Jesus was referring to when Nicodemus, a ruler of the Jews, and a Pharisee (the supposed religious authorities and teachers of the Jews) came in the night to question Him. Jesus told him:

> "unless one is born again, he cannot see the kingdom of God." (John 3:3)

Jesus is not speaking of the hackneyed cliché people irreverently toss around; He is describing a supernatural encounter with God, one that fundamentally changes a person from the inside out. To paraphrase, you had a physical birth, but now a second one (hence, being "born again") is required, a spiritual birth. This is how God will give faith to His creation. Faith will be birthed in their hearts by His own life-generating love and power:

> Every good thing given and every perfect gift is from above, coming down from the Father of lights, with whom there is no variation or shifting shadow. (James 1:17)

So, God has a gift for us, but the gift must be *received* for one to own it. The Holy Spirit is a gentleman in the sense that He will prompt you and woo you, but He will not force your hand. He will not demand you take the gift. He is waiting for you to tell Him what you want. After all, when someone offers you a gift, you have to exert some effort to reach out and take it from them. Faith must grow some legs.

My favorite real-world illustration of faith is the "chair," which begins with the observation that faith is not necessarily a mystical concept; it's really something we practice every day even though we don't call it faith. The first step is to point to a chair and ask the person if they believe the chair will hold them up if they sit in it. If they say "yes," then you point out to them that they have just made a "faith" decision. They believe the chair will hold them up, and hence they have decided to sit (trust) in it. Conclusion: The primary factor in making a faith judgment is evaluating the trustworthiness of the *object* of your faith—in this case, the chair. Of secondary importance is how much faith you alone possess. When we understand this, the primary tenet of faith, then the overall picture begins to come more into focus.

Thus, the idea of faith only makes sense when there is a benefactor involved, one who is capable of rewarding our faith and has our welfare in mind. It's a concept we instinctively learn in childhood if, hopefully, we have someone who cares for us, namely our parents or our caretaker. Yes, we may be born with a certain temperament, but much of our personality, social skills, and philosophy of life are products of the way (and the extent to which) they were able to love and nurture us. In that sense, they are our introduction to living by the concept of faith because whether we realize it or not, we are profoundly shaped by what they did or did not provide for us. They were our first benefactors.

If faith is largely dependent upon the quality and the character of the benefactor, it then stands to reason that the most important life decisions we make will revolve around whom we choose to put our faith in, right? Who we choose as our friends, spouse, and even employer, will dramatically affect the quality of our lives. Taking that one step further, *who* or *what* we choose to be our "god" will have the greatest impact on our lives.

My father (and he would have been the first to admit this) chose to worship **work** as his god. He had dreams of owning his own business and becoming the best at what he did. He achieved that dream. Unfortunately, "work" did not prove to be a very worthy god to worship, for work was not very concerned about his wife, daughter, and two sons—all of whom needed much more of him and his time. Fortunately for all of us, my dad realized that work had failed him as a god, and he turned instead to the God of the Bible, who would profoundly affect his priorities in the latter half of his life. He had spent his working life trying to get and/or achieve something that would make him feel good about himself, but what he found was not what he nor the people in his circle of influence needed.

We are designed to be fulfilled by the person of God—not by possessions, achievements, or prosperity—but by God *alone*. Even your deepest friendships, as rewarding and satisfying as they may be, are not a sufficient replacement for your relationship with God.

Once we decide to begin moving past ourselves and take that first step toward knowing the Lord, He will begin the process of revealing Himself to us. I once considered the ideas of God and faith to be purely abstract concepts, but as God began to respond to my seeking heart, I truly believe the Bible was the instrument He used to awaken faith in my soul. Romans 10:17 says this:

> So faith comes from **hearing,** and hearing **by the word of Christ.**

That verse meant absolutely nothing to me until I began to read the Bible and hear it taught on a regular basis. I didn't understand everything I read, but fortunately, I was in an environment (a men's Bible study) where I was able to ask questions of people who were more familiar with the information. I also attended a Sunday School class where the Bible was being taught on a regular basis.

To be clear, I was never put under compulsion by anyone to seek out answers from the Bible or from "church," nor was I brainwashed or manipulated in any way. My observations and conclusions were wholly my own. Did God supernaturally enable me to understand what I was hearing? Undoubtedly He did, allowing His truth to unfold at exactly the pace I could digest it. Be aware, though, that 1 Corinthians 2:14 makes a very clear statement regarding the ability of the nonbeliever to comprehend God's Word without His assistance:

> But a natural man does not accept the things of the Spirit of God, for they are foolishness to him; and he cannot understand them because they are spiritually appraised.

Over the course of three to four months, I was struck by one thing in particular: Although the Bible was composed of 66 different "books" written over a span of approximately 1,500 to 2,000 years, it was undergirded by a remarkable consistency and congruity I couldn't help but notice. It did not contradict itself. It was grounded in history.

I also noticed the glib honesty with which its heroes and villains were depicted. Nothing was sugarcoated. People were portrayed with both their virtues *and* flaws on full display. It was full of the kind of incidental life "details" you would find only in a genuine manuscript—specifically, the details of real, flesh-and-blood relationships, such as Paul's salutation to his protégé Timothy in 2 Timothy 4:9-22.

One of the events that formed my faith occurred when the pastor at the church I was attending preached a sermon about the two thieves who were crucified together with Jesus. He identified one of these men as a skeptic who mocked Jesus (as did others in the crowd) by insisting, since Jesus was supposedly the Messiah, that He save Himself and merely get down off the cross of His own volition. The other thief was far more humble and begged Jesus to "remember me when you come in your kingdom" (Luke 23:42). This caught me by surprise because I realized at once the dichotomy of the unbelieving heart—and the believing one.

Which man was I?

God's Word identified this dilemma in my own heart, and I was forced to examine where I stood in relation to the historical account I was reading. Straddling the fence was no longer an option. There was a choice to be made.

If you choose to believe in God, be prepared to encounter some challenges along the way. Believing in God does not remove all your problems and put you on easy street. In fact, just the opposite is true, and believers will encounter not only opposition from people but also opposition from an entire cultural mindset that makes it a challenge to remain positive. At times, it's a struggle to maintain a loving, nonjudgmental attitude toward those whose voices make up that oppositional attitude and to simultaneously cope with living in the midst of a pleasure-loving, increasingly fragmented culture that seems to be screaming back at us:

"Where is your God?"

This inward battle can eat away at virtues like kindness and charity, creating an emotional minefield that must be navigated one challenge at a time. The Bible says I should "return good for evil" and not take my own vengeance, so we must discipline ourselves to suspend judgment and hold our tongue when we encounter adversarial situations.

The believer is caught in a unique tension that most nonbelievers cannot easily appreciate. We cannot judge those who don't believe, yet we are called to stand up for what we believe is right, moral, and ethical. God's laws must form the basis of our worldview, and that means we have a responsibility to stand for biblical principles even if society in general is hostile to those ideas. In other words, we must involve ourselves in the political process; we must vote for those candidates and ideas that most reflect the standards we believe God is calling us to live by.

Sooner or later, most believers will encounter the familiar argument of separation of church and state, but it is often misunderstood and misapplied by those who use it to attack faith. The Constitution of the United States says that "Congress shall make no law respecting an establishment of religion, or prohibiting the free exercise thereof...."[6] In other words, the government cannot sponsor a religion and/or mandate the practice of any particular religion, nor can it deliberately stop you from practicing religion.

However, those who use this argument to try to keep "religious" principles from being enacted into law or to deny believers freedom of expression in the political arena conveniently overlook one obvious reality: The government is made up of individuals, **all of whom are beholden to a set of beliefs of some kind**.

In fact, whether they believe in God or not, every individual is "religious," for what is religion but a "system" of belief, and every single person erects his or her own internal system with its own boundaries of behavior, standards of judgment, and consequences for violating said boundaries. All of us have some internal code defining what we consider acceptable and unacceptable behavior, right? It's a matter of where you draw the lines. Is lying acceptable? What about infidelity in a marriage? Well, it depends on what I *personally* define "infidelity" to be.

We have these boundaries and principles we want to see respected, even if we haven't written them down or articulated them in public. If we truly think we are beholden to no idea, no principle, or no standard, then we are deceiving ourselves. We are engaged in making and cataloging judgments every single conscious moment, constantly compiling a dossier of positions on various subjects, and thus erecting our own internal system of values, whether we acknowledge it or not.

So, each and every one of us is "religious"; we just don't call it by that name. Unfortunately, in today's social climate, the context of the word seems no different from that of a racial slur. This word is used to conveniently label people who believe in the existence of God. It is used to denigrate, marginalize, and then demonize them, but in reality, religion is a concept all human beings live and operate by. Do I believe that abortion is acceptable, i.e., it does not violate my internal code of behavior? Then I have a *system of belief*. I am *religious*.

Separation of church and state, then, while it does limit the action of an *organization* (in the case of the U.S. Constitution, "Congress"), has no application to or jurisdiction over what the *individual* believes to be true. In fact, *every* person who participates in the government brings their religion, their system, with them. The fact that some employ a system of belief that includes God while also participating in government is inevitable, but it is not a violation of the Constitution, nor is it a violation of anyone else's rights, for each of us is "legislating" morality in our own heart every single day of our existence.

As citizens we are called upon to do it under the guise of voting for laws and our representatives in government. A legislator, which is essentially what we are as a citizen and voter, is called to represent the ideas and beliefs we believe to be true and just. We are expected to represent our conscience, and if our conscience is informed by a belief in a higher power, then so be it. The Constitution does not disqualify the believer from participating in government simply because he or she subscribes to belief in the authority of God.

Therein lies the tension between public posture and personal belief. This unique tension usually escapes the notice of the typical nonbeliever; managing it is often beyond the spiritual capabilities of all but the most mature believers. It's no easy task to strike the balance between standing up for your beliefs and, yet, in the same breath, not judging those who choose to disregard or even ridicule those beliefs.

That is an ongoing struggle for most believers, myself included.

6
PRAYER: THE BRIDGE TO FAITH

TO A GREAT extent, the ability to maintain faith in the midst of our increasingly oppositional culture will hinge on how strong our connection is to the Lord. There is no question He can fulfill His end of the deal, but can we maintain our posture in the midst of so much opposition? We need to stay connected to other believers and to the Lord, so we must rely on our prayer life to keep us tethered to the source of our strength.

There are certain qualities of heart we must bring to the game if we want to sustain spiritual strength and finish the race well. The parable of the widow and the unjust judge in Luke 18:1-8 offers several principles we need to incorporate into our communion with God:

> Now He was telling them a parable to show that **at all times** they ought to pray and **not to lose heart**, saying, "In a certain city there was a judge who did not fear God and did not respect man. There was a widow in that city, and **she kept coming to him**, saying, 'Give me legal protection from my opponent.' For a while he was unwilling; but afterward he said to himself, 'Even though I do not fear God nor respect man, yet because this widow bothers me, I will give her legal protection, otherwise by continually coming she will wear me out.'" And the Lord said, "Hear what the unrighteous judge said; now, will not God bring about justice for His elect **who cry to Him day and night**, and will He delay long over them? I tell you that He will bring about justice for them quickly. **However, when the Son of Man comes, will He find faith on the earth?**"

First, we notice that prayer is for "all times," as verse 1 says. To confine prayer strictly to spiritual settings or to practice it only on certain occasions is to relegate it to strictly ancillary status in our lives. First Thessalonians 5:17 says to "pray without ceasing." I wonder what we could discover about God (and ourselves) if we were to take that verse literally. Whether we are in need, anxious, fearful, excited, or simply content—whatever the circumstances—we should be praying. We have a God with inexhaustible resources, and if we can line up our will with His will, then He can bless us and use us to bless others.

Remember, **God is our benefactor**. He delights in giving gifts to His children, and we must keep looking to Him to provide for us. We must fortify our hearts against any doubt or unbelief by doing as the widow did: She kept bringing her requests to the judge, and she was not discouraged by his indifference to her or by his disrespect for God. She persisted; *she kept coming*. Jesus, of course, is the opposite of the unrighteous judge, who only granted the widow justice because he was annoyed by her constant requests to be protected from her enemies.

God delights in listening and responding to our prayers, and He sees our persistence as a demonstration of faith in His goodness. He delights in seeing us wearing out a path to His throne room. We need to be more persistent, like we were as kids, pulling at our fathers' pants and asking, "Why, Daddy, why?" As verse 7 says, when we "cry to Him day and night," He will bring about justice and He will protect us from our enemies. What happens, though, when God seems to tarry over His answer? We may grow tired of repeating the prayer, and our pleas to God may become bogged down into routine recitation.

One of the most daunting challenges a believer faces is to renew our flagging spirit, to refocus and transition from weariness to infusing our prayers with passion and energy. Periodically, you have to pump up the volume and pray harder, with more zeal and passion, and if the answer still tarries and you lapse into the routine, then once again, regroup and reenergize your pleas to God. Put your *whole* heart into it. Cry out to the Lord.

Some of us approach prayer like we're discussing the weather. You have to get down to it and dig deeper in the well that is within your heart; bring up the passion springs of zeal when you fall on your knees before the Lord. It often helps to shout when you pray. (Remember the movie *War Room*?[7] See it, if you haven't already). Be ferocious, be fervent, and be fierce, especially when nothing seems to be happening.

After all, you are talking to God Almighty.

There is another seemingly opposite approach that can also be beneficial to our communion with God. Perhaps the drag on our prayer life is all the noise in our world. We sometimes suffer from an inability to slow down and sit still long enough to unhurriedly bask in God's presence. We need calm water.

As we dialogue with Him in prayer, we must cultivate a *listening* heart; we must learn how to become quiet in His presence so we can hear Him speak to us. If we fail to cultivate this serenity, the clamor and noise of the world can drown out God's still, small voice, and we will miss out on what He has for us. We become bystanders instead of participants in the Lord's work here on earth. This state of mind can rob us of our joy.

We need to guard against one tendency that can sabotage our faith: We can land ourselves into some trouble when our expectations run ahead of God's timing. Will He answer our prayers? Yes, but we must not forget that the ***timing*** of His answer is exclusively His province. Hence, the exhortation "not to lose heart," in verse 1, which is essential when the answer to our prayer seems to tarry. God's challenge to us is to wait for Him in persistent confidence and to leave the timing and outcome of our prayers to His discretion. Of course, one contradiction we face is that we sometimes pray for (and want) items or outcomes *not* within the providential will of God. There's no getting around it and no easy way to explain it. At times, our prayers are not answered the way we wish them to be, and we are left to wrestle with disappointment.

We can mitigate that temporary struggle or at least learn to manage it by altering our perspective on prayer. It's such a temptation to present your prayers to God as if it were a question-and-answer session with a tour guide. We have conditioned ourselves, especially in the United States, to expect instant answers to our problems. If the doctor can fix what ails us with a pill, God should be able to do the same, right?

But the spiritual reality of prayer is so very different. It's not about the answer, per se; it's more about the conversation, the process of talking to and then listening to God, of "exploring" the subject with the Lord and waiting patiently for His feedback. Enjoy the process, and along the way, cultivate your *relationship* with Him. While it would be nice if we heard Him speak audibly to us, that's not His usual method of disclosure. The Lord's plan, whatever it may look like, may take a while to unfold in human time. He has to arrange the circumstances, shape the hearts of those involved, and then wait for people's will to line up with His own.

From our viewpoint, all this takes place in real time. In God time, He already knows what events need to occur and when, but if He merely zapped everything right as we want it to be, then life (and faith) as we know it would be meaningless. Our input and presence would be totally unnecessary. God, however, chooses to work through people most of the time. People can be a little slow on the uptake, a little stubborn, and a little slow to fall in line with God's will.

If your prayers go continually unanswered, it may be wise to conduct a periodic spiritual inventory of your motives. In James 4:3, God says this:

> You ask and do not receive because you ask with wrong motives, so that you may spend it on your pleasures.

We need to develop the habit of examining our hearts to see if we may be praying for that which represents the fulfillment of a selfish desire. Even prayers we send up for other people can be subtle in their selfishness, such as when we pray for someone's behavior or attitude to change, but we ourselves are not willing to take a look at how our actions are affecting the relationship. Asking God to change the other person is far easier than doing the hard work required to effect change in ourselves.

Or it could be that we simply want what we want. The craving we have for pleasure can be insatiable. At times, we approach God like a kid in a candy store: "I'll have one of everything, please!" We need to take that inventory of our motives seriously so we can present a pure heart to the Lord. That's also why reading God's Word is so important because it is *"living and active and able to judge the thoughts and intentions of the heart"* (Hebrews 4:12).

We need it to keep the pleasure-loving part of our souls in check. His Word "is piercing as far as the division of soul and spirit, of both joints and marrow," and thus it aids us in separating our "soulish," self-satisfying desires from the desires of our spirit, which hopefully are a product of God's Spirit touching us and filling us with His own set of motives and desires.

In examining scripture, we find there are other reasons prayers may go unanswered. The following chart gives some examples from the Bible and explanations why these prayers may be hindered or not heard.

As it states in the chart, *"**Dipsuchos**"* is the Greek word used to describe the believer who has "two souls," or whose affections are divided between, for example, pleasing God and gaining something for themselves.[8]

Reason	Reference	Explanation
1. Hypocritical	Matthew 6:5	Praying to be seen (approved) by others. Valuing the approval of man over God's approval.
2. Vain Repetition	Matthew 6:7	Repeating the same phrases/sentences over and over again Your prayers must come from the heart if you wish to incur God's favor.
3. Double-Minded; Doubting	James 1:5-8	**"Dipsuchos"** is the Greek word used to describe the believer who has "two souls," or whose affections are divided between, for example, pleasing God and gaining something for themselves.
4. Wrongly Motivated	James 4:3	Prayers that are selfishly motivated Seeking only one's own benefit or pleasure
5. Unreconciled Relationships	I Peter 3:7	This verse adjures us to live in harmony with our wives, "so that your prayers may not be hindered." It can certainly be extended to include all relationships, which, as a general rule, should be marked by reconciliation, understanding, and forgiveness.

In addition, we need to make sure we are not "coveting" a particular answer to prayer. The goal is not to mark down how many satisfactory answers we receive from the Lord but to become a channel of His will through prayer, to become a conduit of His life-changing love and power. If we are coveting a particular answer, then we face a grave danger, since coveting can deeply affect the health of our hearts. Proverbs 13:12 says:

> Hope deferred makes the heart sick, but desire fulfilled is a tree of life.

Better to have the hope in our hearts keyed to the expressed will of God, rather than to unchecked emotions or misplaced desires. If we are in God's Word daily, He will have input into our heart; He will be shaping it and molding it; He will fill it with that which He knows is necessary for us to fulfill the purposes He has prepared for us. Beware of any affection you have for someone or something that is greater than your affection for the Lord. Those affections, left unexamined and unchecked, can potentially make your heart sick.

This pattern is often played out in romantic relationships. If we become attached to or involved with a person who does not share our faith in Christ, we may end up paying a very steep price for that involvement. If our partner is pulling in a different direction from our own, the chances of a sustaining, unified relationship are not good. We need to be diligent in evaluating his or her true spiritual condition because many people say they "believe in God," but our Lord wants so much more for us than merely a commitment to a religion or to attending church. We need to make sure the other person is pursuing a *relationship* with Christ.

Yes, it's nice if our partner goes to church and reads the Bible with us, but that alone is not enough. We should make sure he or she exhibits a passion for Christ before we become emotionally involved. If we choose to ignore God in this area, then we should *beware* because this decision may lead to some deep emotional scarring, not only for us, but also for the other person. Occasionally, the relationship works out and the other person becomes a genuine believer; more often than not, it doesn't, and the results can lead to a spiritual or emotional train wreck that can affect the rest of our lives.

Nevertheless, the possibility of falling in love with someone who does not share our faith in Christ still exists. It happens. But should we marry that person? In 2 Corinthians 6:14, the Apostle Paul states this:

> Do not be bound together with unbelievers; for what partnership have righteousness and lawlessness, or what fellowship has light with darkness?

Here, God is giving us a general command that applies to all situations, including marriage. We romanticize marriage and ideas such as "falling in love" and "meeting your soul mate," but for the believer, the decision to marry someone is still *secondary* to his or her relationship with Christ. We must never allow any person or any *thing* to supplant our allegiance to our Lord.

If we choose to marry a nonbeliever, we are putting our relationship with Christ at risk because our spouse may attempt to pull us away from Him, be it through aggressive resistance or passive indifference. Moreover, the relationship will be undermined by differing goals and lifestyles. How do we spend our time? How do we spend our money? Don't be surprised if conflict ends up dominating the marriage under these circumstances.

This principle has a very specific precedent in the Old Testament. Prior to the Israelites entering the Promised Land,

Moses forewarns the people regarding the danger of becoming unequally yoked to the various people groups they were about to displace:

> "When the LORD your God brings you into the land where you are entering to possess it, and clears away many nations before you... and when the LORD your God delivers them before you and you defeat them, then you shall utterly destroy them. You shall make no covenant with them and show no favor to them. Furthermore, you shall not intermarry with them; you shall not give your daughters to their sons, nor shall you take their daughters for your sons. For they will turn your sons away from following Me to serve other gods; then the anger of the LORD will be kindled against you and He will quickly destroy you." (Deuteronomy 7:1-4)

The importance of this decision cannot be underestimated. The marriage relationship is holy and sacred and should not to be entered into lightly or without forethought. If we want to make good, sound, life-altering decisions such as choosing a like-minded life partner, we must keep our lives centered around Christ. This focus on Him will ensure that our hearts are "good" soil, ready to receive and cultivate whatever desires God wants to plant there.

This is why Jesus ends the widow's story with the question:

"When the Son of Man comes, will He find faith on the earth?"

He is challenging us to remain focused on Him as we wait for His plan to unfold in our lives. He knows our tendency is to become discouraged, to give up, and to falter if our desires are not fulfilled. However, we must not be like the disciples who could not stay awake and on-watch in the Garden of Gethsemane as Jesus prayed before His crucifixion. We are called to stay on high alert for the Lord, to maintain a posture of prayer in our hearts while we wait for His timing to be fulfilled.

My cousin Jim, who was like an older brother to me, did not come to know the Lord until he was 57 years old. At that time, I had been praying for him off and on for almost 30 years. His parents had done the same but for far longer. Despite the long wait, God got his attention at exactly the perfect time, which occurred when circumstances and his life experience conspired to make his heart tender and receptive to God's offer of salvation.

We need to endure in prayer, to never give up on God. Not only does change take time, but if a person you are praying for is resisting God, then he or she may be delaying God's work through the Spirit. Rest assured, though, that God does not give up on that person, and neither should we.

The key is to remember we are called to keep watch; to endure; to lay aside every sin, doubt, and fear; and to focus only on what God can provide.

7

THE AUTHOR OF FAITH

> Therefore, since we have so great a cloud of witnesses surrounding us, let us also lay aside every encumbrance and the sin which so easily entangles us, and let us run with endurance the race that is set before us, fixing our eyes on Jesus, the *author* and *perfecter* of faith, who for the joy set before Him endured the cross, despising the shame, and has sat down at the right hand of the throne of God. (Hebrews 12:1-2)

RELIANCE UPON GOD is the calling card of the believer. He is our supernatural sustainer, and everything we have is from His hand, including faith itself. Jesus Christ is the originator of faith (verse 2), the "archegos" (Greek) of, first, our belief in Him, and then our belief in His provisional hand acting in and through us. In *contrast* to the *archegos*, "one may be the cause of something but not the beginning."[9] *Archegos* denotes not only the "cause," but also the beginner, the founder, the first possessor, the inventor, the originator, the progenitor, the *author*. This is a singular position Christ alone holds; He will not give His glory to another—not to any other prophet, not to any so-called religion. He will not shrink back from the responsibility of the *archegos*, which is to model His invention for His subjects.

When a person says "yes" to Jesus Christ, faith is the first "gift" he or she receives. When this impartation of faith occurs, there is also an impartation of the Holy Spirit. He will enter your being, and you will be filled with the Spirit of Christ. You will then have the same faith at your disposal that Jesus expressed when He was tempted by the devil to turn away from God, His Father; the same faith required to sweat drops of blood as He prayed, *"…yet not My will, but Yours be done"* (Luke 22:42) before he was betrayed by His own disciples. It is the same faith it took to endure persecution and unjust treatment by His own family.

Not only is He the Author of faith, He is also the "Perfecter" (verse 2), the "Teleiotes" (Greek), the one who completes the race, the one who endures to receive the prize.[10] This is exactly the goal God sets before us: to run the race and to finish it well. The Apostle Paul, a man who wrote a good portion of the New Testament from a prison cell, summarized it so well:

> I have fought the good fight, I have finished the course, I have kept the faith; in the future there is laid up for me the crown of righteousness, which the Lord, the righteous Judge, will award to me on that day; and not only to me, but also to all who have loved His appearing. (2 Timothy 4:7-8)

Faith is not merely a good idea; it is the prize; it is the end game; it is worth fighting for, worth running and finishing the race for, and worth keeping watch over. It is our most treasured tool with which we have to work, our pipeline to the Lord. God means to nurture and strengthen it if we will only confide in Him everything that matters to us. Keeping that confidence is our secret weapon, ready to be revealed when we most need it, when temptation is facing us down, or when life seems too difficult to bear. We must guard it with all of our being, nurture it, stimulate it, challenge it, and share it. We should do everything possible to sustain it and strengthen it. To live by faith is to live in complete dependence upon the Lord, to have confidence in His strength, not our own:

> Now faith is the assurance of things hoped for, the conviction of things not seen... And without faith, it is impossible to please Him, for he who comes to God must believe that He is and that He is a rewarder of those who seek Him. (Hebrews 11:1, 6)

Faith can be a daunting concept to some of us because, technically speaking, it belongs to the unseen world, the spirit world. You can see the results of it, but you cannot view the process itself. When we have hard, visible evidence in front of us that testifies to its origin or cause, we have no problem believing something. But when it requires us to trust in an invisible agent, even one who claims to be acting on our behalf, we are not so easily convinced.

It requires a shift in perspective, one that is willing to acknowledge the possibility that there is not only a power greater than ourselves, but that this power is acting in our best interests, and, furthermore, possesses an infallible moral character. Try thinking of your prayers as your contribution to this partnership—an exchange of ideas and concerns with God. In this case, your partner happens to possess unlimited resources, and He has plans for you, plans to make your life fulfilling and rich. This God must simultaneously be perfectly loving and perfectly just. No creature can go unloved, no right can go unrewarded, and no wrong can go unpunished. To be worthy of our trust, He must exceed all human limitations. The God of the Bible claims to be unique, in that He alone claims to have authority over all creation:

> "I am the Lord, and there is no other; besides Me there is no God. I will gird you, though you have not known Me; that men may know from the rising to the setting of the sun that there is no one besides Me. I am the Lord, and there is no other." (Isaiah 45:5-6)

What evidence is there for the claims He makes? First of all, there is the evidence of creation itself, which the Apostle Paul describes in succinct detail:

> For since the creation of the world His invisible attributes, His eternal power and divine nature, have been clearly seen, being understood through what has been made, so that they are without excuse. For even though they knew God, they did not honor Him as God or give thanks, but they became futile in their speculations, and their foolish heart was darkened. Professing to be wise, they became fools, and exchanged the glory of the incorruptible God for an image in the form of corruptible man

> and of birds and four-footed animals and crawling creatures. (Romans 1:20-23)

There is also the evidence that resides in the hearts and minds of believers everywhere. If you are want to move toward God, I urge you to seek out a mentor, someone who has walked with God for at least 10 to 15 years, and absorb his or her stories of God's life-sustaining power and provision. Certainly you can talk to new believers, too, but from them you may only get the initial first rush of excitement and fascination with discovering that God actually exists. From the experienced believer, you will receive solid evidence testifying to God's continuing action in his or her life. Be on the lookout for a mentor of this ilk, whose life is marked by devotion to the Lord.

Having walked with God for some time now, I can testify to His love and provision. I can honestly say that I have yet to see a single word of the Bible disproved, and I have gathered a cumulative body of evidence—some of it indisputably supernatural—that testifies to God's presence here on earth. Part of the joy of walking through life with the Lord lies in accumulating a living journal of your interaction with Him, and that is a treasure meant to be shared with others who would seek to know the Lord.

There are many other passages where the God of the Bible proclaims His preeminence and singularity as the one true God. He alone claims to have the power to "assure" our faith and that He is the one who will reward us for our faith. Again, in Matthew 7:7, He states that He is the one who will answer our prayers and satisfy our souls:

> "Ask, and it shall be given to you; seek, and you shall find; knock, and it shall be opened to you… Or what man is there among you who, when his son asks for a loaf, will give him a stone? Or if he asks for a fish, he will not give him a snake, will he? If you then, being evil, know how to give good gifts to your

children, how much more will your Father who is in heaven give what is good to those who ask Him!" (Matthew 7:7, 9-11)

If God is the assurer of our faith and custodian of our prayers, our role is to provide trust—the "conviction of things not seen," as Hebrews 11:1 describes it. To do that, our focus has to be on our benefactor and His ability to come through each and every time. We have to recognize that however God answers our prayers, it is "good" in the truest sense because it reflects His will. We may not see an immediate answer to a specific prayer, yet that may be part of God's plan as He works to develop our faith "muscle." We have to see these delayed answers and anything else life throws at us as normal, which is the act of faith on our part. We have to believe that God is in control of the spirit world, the unseen world:

> For momentary, light affliction is producing for us an eternal weight of glory far beyond all comparison, while we look not at the things which are seen, but at the things which are not seen; for the things which are seen are temporal, but the things which are not seen are eternal. (2 Corinthians 4:17-18)

Hence, we must look at the world through the same lens God uses: the lens of eternity. If our gaze is fixed only on the temporal (the present state of things), only on what we can consciously observe in people, then our prayers will be anemic and shortsighted. If we only pray for someone to be healed or to find a better job, we are merely praying for "relief" from a difficulty or situation, but God is not always looking to relieve someone of their temporary discomfort. He may be using circumstances and discomfort to the outer person to effect change in the inner person.

If, then, we see as God sees, then we will *observe* someone's *present* needs, but we will *pray* for his or her *eternal* needs. Sometimes, for example, you may encounter people who are given to throwing a pity party over every little personal slight or difficulty they encounter in life, and they are prone to miscast everyone as an enemy in their personal dramas. In this case, we should not be praying for this "victim's" enemies to repent but rather for our friend to understand that everything people do or say is not about them! Pray they come to a deeper understanding of human nature as well as a true understanding of how God views His children.

In a situation like this one, it is beneficial to pray for this person to not personalize everything, to adjust his or her expectations of people, and to not be so surprised when someone mistreats him or her or says something inconsiderate. People will be people, and much of the time they are not thinking before they speak. Do not expect others to always treat you perfectly; you will be miserably disappointed and bitter if you do. Instead, you must be ready to respond with grace and forgiveness if necessary. This is an example of how we can pray for the "inner" person—the eternal person.

If God changes the person on the inside, then his or her behavior will eventually follow suit.

8
GOD OF LOVE AND GOD OF JUDGMENT

In this is love, not that we loved God, but that He loved us and sent His Son to be the propitiation for our sins. (1 John 4:10)

For God will bring every act to judgment, everything which is hidden, whether it is good or evil. (Ecclesiastes 12:14)

SOME RELIGIONS PORTRAY God as the great smiter, the harsh taskmaster, or the aloof pinsetter who dwells in unapproachable splendor while we humans are left with the unenviable task of sorting out life here on planet earth while still managing to please this arbitrary, capricious, often malevolent supreme being who not only doesn't love us but actively disdains our pursuit of happiness by making rules aimed at taking away our fun and afflicting us with unnecessary suffering and pain. I could go on and on, right?

I don't think I'm exaggerating when I say this is pretty much most people's default perception of God as the Great Joy-Sucker in the Sky. Truthfully, though, if one allows a view of God to be shaped exclusively by what takes place here on earth, then it's not hard to see how one could adopt this perspective. After all, life is almost never easy for most of us and for some of us, it has been, is now, or will soon contain its fair share of trouble—and that's just for those of us living in relative prosperity. What about those whose physical suffering alone makes our "problems" translucently pale in comparison? Doesn't God care about them? Does He care only about the prosperity seekers living our lives of ease here in America?

But that would be misstating it, wouldn't it, because honestly, much of the misery extant in this world is of humankind's own making. We, not God, start wars. We, not God, ruin relationships. We, not God, want what doesn't belong to us.

So, why are we so quick to blame "God" when something goes wrong? Ever notice that when a bad situation happens, we have this peculiar tendency to attribute all the responsibility to "God"?

Why did You let that happen, God?

Why don't You stop that person from doing what he is doing, God?

It's almost a reflexive response, an involuntary reaction that arises out of our souls, an indignant reaction directed at someone we think should be looking out for us. Yet, we often fail to thank God or give Him credit when life is going well. In fact, rather than stop to earnestly thank the Lord for providing for us, we are more likely to double down on the good stuff and go looking for more of it. People use the phrase, "Thank God" all the time, but it's meaningless, content-less, to most of us, nothing more than an idiomatic expression of relief we spout when we happen to notice that things could be much worse.

This blame game we play with Him should give us pause for thought. Some claim God doesn't even exist, but we still have this almost innate tendency to blame Him when life takes a negative turn. Moreover, we like holding on to the idea of having someone watching out for us whom we can hold responsible for life's pratfalls, but we don't like the idea of being accountable for our actions to that same person. We like to run our own show. I believe that's commonly referred to as "self-centeredness."

This tendency we have to self-direct our lives gets us into trouble quite often, especially when we find ourselves idle, not engaged, doing whatever appeals to us at the moment. In reality, we often avoid doing that which we are either responsible for—be it at work, home, or elsewhere—or find more onerous than enjoyable. Witness King David, ruler of Israel, and the manner in which he entraps himself:

> Then it happened in the spring, **at the time when kings go out to battle**, that David sent Joab and his servants with him and all Israel, and they destroyed the sons of Ammon and besieged Rabbah. **But David stayed at Jerusalem**. (2 Samuel 11:1)

At first glimpse, it appears as if the mission was accomplished and the enemy was defeated, but that was not the real issue. David, not Joab, should have been out and about leading his army. David was in Jerusalem, but in the wrong place at the wrong time, and temptation came to pay him a visit. He had unwittingly placed himself in spiritual danger by abdicating his post as commander of the army. God can help us course-correct if we come to our senses quickly enough, but often as not, it's too late in the game to extricate ourselves from these types of situations.

David's situation is not unique, for the Bible is littered with examples of people shirking their God-given responsibilities. What does surprise us, though, is that we don't expect a man of David's character, who is described in 1 Samuel 13:14, as "a man after His [God's] own heart" to succumb so easily to sin. Yet, it happens in an instant. When he sees Bathsheba, he is *hooked*:

> Now when evening came David arose from his bed and walked around on the roof of the king's house, and from the roof he saw a woman bathing; and the woman was very beautiful in appearance. So David sent and inquired about the woman.... (2 Samuel 11:2-3a)

How long did it take David to make his fateful decision to pursue Bathsheba? Maybe it was instantly, maybe he pondered his plan for a while, but the time required is inconsequential, for he had already lost the battle by being somewhere he wasn't supposed to be.

His eventual sexual conquest of Bathsheba—and subsequent and successful plan to have her husband sacrificed and killed on the front lines of a battle David should have been leading—is a grotesque and ruthless example of selfishness. God disciplined David for that sin. He suffered not only the embarrassment of God pointing out his sin through a close friend, but he also had to witness the death of his infant son by Bathsheba.

Throughout the next several years, his other sons were constantly at odds with each other, and one of them even attempted to usurp David's own throne! In 2 Samuel 12:9-11, we are told of God's judgment upon David's sin:

> "Why have you despised the word of the Lord by doing evil in His sight? You have struck down Uriah the Hittite with the sword, have taken his wife to be your wife, and have killed him with the sword of the sons of Ammon. Now therefore, the sword shall never depart from your house because you have despised Me and have taken the wife of Uriah the Hittite to be your wife.' Thus says the Lord, 'Behold, I will raise up evil against you from your own household; I will even take your wives before your eyes and give them to your companion, and he will lie with your wives in broad daylight."

Although David immediately repented of his sin after being confronted with God's edict through Nathan the prophet, he still had to endure a lifetime of turmoil and strife in his family. He did not escape the consequences of his barbaric misstep. God forgave him, yes, but here we also see God directly administering both the discipline and the punishment for his sin.

In fact, throughout the Old Testament we witness God disciplining and punishing not only His enemies and the enemies of Israel but also His people directly from His own hand. At times, He wiped out entire cities and tribes of people who opposed His purposes through Israel. But Israel could be even more problematic than its enemies at times. God called His own people "stubborn" and "stiff-necked," and they were constantly being disciplined for their failure to obey their Lord.

The story of Korah's rebellion in the sixteenth chapter of the Book of Numbers is but one of many examples of Israel's disobedience. Korah was a priest, a member of the tribe of Levi, who challenged the leadership credentials of Moses and Aaron, both of whom God had appointed as leaders over Israel. Korah believed he was as qualified as Moses to lead God's people. Moses instructed Korah and his followers to assemble outside their tents on the following morning to see how God felt about the situation:

> Moses said, "By this you shall know that the Lord has sent me to do all these deeds; for this is not my doing. If these men die the death of all men or if they suffer the fate of all men, then the Lord has not sent me. But if the Lord brings about an entirely new thing and the ground opens its mouth and swallows them up with all that is theirs, and they descend alive into Sheol, then you will understand that these men have spurned the Lord." As he finished speaking all these words, the ground that was under them split open; and the earth opened its mouth and swallowed them up, and their households, and all the men who belonged to Korah with their possessions. (Numbers 16:28-32)

Note that Korah's disobedience also proved fatal not only to himself and his followers and family, but also to the families of Dathan and Abiram (see Numbers 16:12-14), who joined Korah in his plot to overthrow Moses and Aaron. There's an obvious lesson for us in this story. We should be wary of thinking that we alone suffer when we disobey the Lord. People who are close to us are affected by our sin, and their relationship with the Lord can be contaminated by *our* failure to heed God's will.

What about the New Testament? The new covenant does not negate God's will to discipline. In fact, it offers evidence to the contrary. Ananias and Sapphira were two believers whose unfortunate encounter with the Lord in the book of Acts should serve notice to us all that God will not be pushed beyond a certain point. This couple sold some land and brought a portion of it to the apostles as an offering. On the surface, this was a seemingly innocent, even noble gesture, and one might even call it commendable, but there is more to the story. The scripture does not spell it out in so many words, but apparently God was not pleased the couple brought only *part* of the money they received from the land sale. In fact, in Acts 5:3-4, Peter responds in this fashion to the gift laid at his feet by Ananias:

> "Ananias, why has Satan filled your heart to lie to the Holy Spirit and to keep back some of the price of the land? While it remained unsold, did it not remain your own? And after it was sold, was it not under your control? Why is it that you have conceived this deed in your heart? You have not lied to men but to God."

The scripture then goes on to say that "as he heard these words, Ananias fell down and breathed his last...." The people standing around this scene were understandably shocked by this outcome. Ananias's wife Sapphira arrived at the scene three hours later, and she also fell dead at Peter's feet. Can you imagine your own response if you had witnessed something like this? The scripture does not spell out exactly how they "lied to God," but we can infer from the outcome there existed a breach of honesty and trust between themselves and the Lord.

This event probably represents some of the most severe discipline we see exercised in the New Testament. Was this harsh of God? Was it fair? I don't know, but it sure makes me think twice about trying to conceal the truth from others and from God.

We understand from this passage that the state of our hearts is of paramount importance to the Lord. We have to maintain integrity in our relationship with Him if He is to trust us with being His ambassadors here on earth. We may lie to and deceive our fellow man, but God is not a man, and neither is He a fool. He is our sovereign God and Father, and we should strive always to be honest and forthright with Him, lest He be forced to resort to more coercive methods to fix our hearts. Tough love is not a problem for Him.

We know from examples like this one that God disciplines those He loves, and He does it for our good, "...that we may share His holiness" (see Hebrews 12:10). Bear in mind, too, that God's ability to accurately discipline us and judge our hearts is not diminished at all by His capacity for love, which is the other facet of His personality we need to grasp. God's love is a perfect representation of His nature and finds its penultimate expression in Christ's sacrificial death on the cross for all mankind—past, present, and future. God's judgment and God's love meet here in perfect harmony, for what is Christ's death but the satisfaction of God's judgment upon sin, and yet also the supremely loving gift of forgiveness and salvation to us? There is no contradiction because both ideas are perfectly realized in this act.

Love, in God's hands, is not merely an idea but a life-giving force that changes us and gives us understanding of what He has done for us. The practical expression of that love will take many different forms in your relationship with the Lord, but be assured, He knows how to touch you in the deepest part of your being. You will often encounter His love in the most ordinary of circumstances. "Ordinary" can be defined in more than one way, but we typically invent clichés to describe the commonplace. Maybe you have a favorite one or, more likely, one you wish would go away. Many have worn out their welcome, but for me the one I currently have blacklisted is: "That's the bomb." It should have passed from this earth long ago, having already overstayed its welcome by several years. Often, though, clichés are clichés because they contain an undeniable element of truth. They have earned the label.

My granddaughter Mariah helped me learn this truth when she was a little lass who stood just over knee-high to me. She had her grandfather wrapped around that little finger of hers in a very big way. As happenstance would have it, I often ended up as her playmate on Saturday or Sunday afternoons while Mom and Nana were napping or running errands. We would invent games to play and entertain each other for hours. Her favorite one we called "fat tummy," which consisted of her stuffing my shirt with pillows and then running around the room and jumping onto my now-fat tummy. As the afternoon wore on, I would occasionally interrupt our fun to tell her I was going to take a break and see what the other adults were doing. She would have none of that, however, and insisted I stay with her and finish our game. I could not say "no" to my persistent little girl.

This was the routine, but one day stands out in my memory. After stuffing my shirt for the third or fourth time, she ran to one end of the room, made the biggest semi-circle toward me she possibly could, and began exclaiming, "Papa Bruce, I love you…Papa Bruce, I love you…" as she rounded the room repeatedly, waving her arms through the air as she went, before finally coming in for a landing. After a few rounds of this, I began to get pretty choked up. Since Mariah is my step-granddaughter, and I do not have biological children of my own, her spontaneous expression of love caught me by surprise. At the time, I was fairly new to grandfather-ing, and this was the first time I had ever heard a child proclaim their love for me. That day, I believe I learned the meaning of the cliché, "Children spell love t-i-m-e." That's one I've never forgotten, and it never gets old.

God gave me a gift that day. I didn't marry until I was 43 years old, so the probability of having my own children was waning by that point in time. I had worked and taught in middle school and high school youth ministry and had spent about seven years being a big brother to two preteen boys, but chances were that I wasn't ever going to have my own family. Yet, who did I end up marrying but my lovely wife Shirley, whose children were grown, married, and beginning to have their own children. For a guy who had always loved kids, this was a godsend, and explains why this experience with Mariah made such an impact on me. She was simply being herself, but through her, God was demonstrating the acuity of His love and His singular ability to satisfy a need that resided in the deepest part of my heart. I have had similar experiences with my other seven grandchildren, and each time it happens, I am reminded of how much He loves me.

You will find that the Lord knows exactly when and where you are in need of a special touch like the one I just described. One of the deepest joys in your relationship with God comes from this accumulation of love, that is, that which He does for you that touches parts of your heart *only He knows about*. Does that mean He has made my life easy? No, but I understand now that my personal comfort was never the objective. What I have discovered is that God has His own special way of "balancing the books," so to speak. He will eventually find a way to fulfill the desires of your heart if you truly love Him.

From this process we can derive lasting satisfaction and a

sense of being valued and understood that will sustain us through all the difficulties life throws at us:

> We have come to know and have believed the love which God has for us. God is love, and the one who abides in love abides in God, and God abides in Him…We love, because He first loved us. (1 John 4:16, 19)

9
CAN WE RELY ON GOD TO TAKE CARE OF US?

SPEAKING OF DIFFICULTIES, how do we manage life when it becomes unmanageable? Some of us are prone to blame God or become angry with Him when prayers aren't answered as quickly as we wish—or seemingly not at all. Blaming God, though, is an oxymoron conceptually because the underlying assumption (never verbalized, of course) is that we are more qualified than God to determine what the future should hold.

Job went through the conundrum of being a righteous, God-fearing man who nevertheless had to endure some extremely harsh blows in his lifetime. He became very angry at God as a result of his sufferings, but in Job, chapters 38 through 42, God helped Job gain some perspective on the immense task of being the one who oversees all of creation. Job eventually realized it was a responsibility he didn't really want, and, moreover, he lacked the qualifications to hold the office in the first place. Yet, God understood Job's pain. He did not abandon Job but counseled him with truth and wisdom.

So, what do we do with the anger, frustration, and pain that result from any one of a myriad of painful events we experience in the course of a lifetime? In the midst of the pain, one of our instincts may be to lash out at God or others because casting blame on something or someone at least gives us some temporary relief from outcomes we can't control. To ask the age-old question "Why?" is to testify to our humanness.

What's funny is that most of us don't ever stop to examine the presumptive reason for even asking that question. We ask it because we believe in the principle of responsibility, and the only reason to believe in such an idea is because in our heart-of-hearts, all of us innately believe that God is "responsible" for caring for us. We want to believe that someone is watching out for us.

Why else would we blame God when something bad happens?

The obvious parallel is in the parent-child relationship. We certainly hold parents responsible for their children's upbringing, and, whether we articulate it or not, I think the vast majority of us subconsciously hold God responsible for our well-being. After all, the Bible presents Him to us as our "Father," and there are numerous descriptions of us as His "children."

Before you scoff at that notion, think carefully about how you view your own parents. For most of us, somewhere along the line, our struggles have led us to scrupulously evaluate their performance on our behalf. That's because our internal compass has a built-in expectation of being cared for and loved on some level, and the statistics bear out exactly how important it is to have at least one parent who meets those needs. Most of us can eventually get past "blaming" our parents for who we are, but nevertheless we recognize the areas in which they failed to give us what we needed. Many of us have even confronted them with those feelings. It's only natural to project those same feelings onto God, who presents Himself to us as "our Father in Heaven."

I submit to you that God loves us in much the same way a *healthy* parent would. He does not save us from every mistake and often uses our failures as teaching opportunities. He gives us what we need, which may be patience, encouragement or frank candor. He practices tough love in the healthiest sense.

He does not shy away from the hard questions; He welcomes them. During the painful times, He is present and comforts us accordingly. In contrast to what our culture has traditionally taught, i.e., rugged individualism and self-sufficiency, He wants us to embrace the frailty of being human by leaning on Him as completely and wholly as possible. Unfortunately, we often misunderstand God's intentions. We allow pain to make us indignant at Him for even allowing such a thing to befall us in the first place.

Job went through this crucible in phases. At first, he was generally accepting of what happened to him, saying at one point, "though He [God] slay me, yet will I hope in Him" (Job 13:15). But later he grew bitter and began to complain to God. It didn't help that his friends accused him of being a victim of God's wrath because of some secret sin he was hiding, which was an untrue assertion. Job had to face the harshness of reality head-on, which is an eventuality for all of us. So buckle up and hold on tight because, all sin aside, life is rough in general. Ultimately, though, God will be there to hold us up when all our resources are exhausted.

My brief, one-year tenure as a full-time missionary spanning 1995 to 1996 brought me up against this very situation. I believed God was calling me to step out in faith and go overseas to teach English. I didn't know exactly what that would look like, but I eventually enlisted with Educational Services International, an organization that placed English teachers all over the world. We spent six weeks in Pasadena, California, going through training, and then we were off to Europe for the school year. I ended up in Komarno, Slovakia, a town of about 35,000 people on the north shore of the Danube River, where the economy was based primarily on shipbuilding. By train, we were an hour northwest of Budapest, Hungary.

When we arrived, my first thought was: *"What in the world am I doing here?"* That was symptomatic of a deep homesickness that set in and stayed with me for some time. I am what you would call a "devout" homebody, and somehow it never occurred to me exactly how out of sync I would feel in a new country, having to make new friends, not speaking the language, and having to learn how to teach English to high school students as I went. I was truly a fish out of water, and I think I walked the streets of Komarno a good three months before it felt like anything even remotely resembling home. In addition to that, before leaving for training, I had just stepped away from a romantic relationship. I'm sure that also affected my outlook on life.

I could not read my Bible. I could not pray. I was a mess as I struggled with the teaching part and the intense feelings of isolation (even though I had a teammate I lived with) that plagued me. I had always prided myself in being able to maintain my relationship with the Lord through prayer and Bible reading, but I couldn't bring myself to do it anymore. I don't know why this was the case, but I felt spiritually *marooned*, if that makes any sense. What is amazing is that my inability to maintain my walk with the Lord did not deter Him from His plans. I found myself in several situations where I had opportunities to share my faith and to help others learn about the Lord.

One night, I was sitting in a local pub with Jean-Pierre, a Canadian who also taught English at my school. Completely out of the blue, he said this to me: "Alright, Bruce, tell me about God." Although I had said little to him about my faith before then, a few months earlier I had purchased a Bible for him, had his name engraved on it, and then presented it to him at dinner one evening. He told me he had been reading it, and then he asked me one of those universal questions almost everyone has pondered at some point in time: "How can a loving God send people to hell?" I tried to explain to him that, yes, God is a God of love, but He is also a God of judgment. Unfortunately, he was having no part of that, and the discussion ended as abruptly as it had started.

God's judgment is a common stumbling point for many people who think it to be unfairly harsh on His part. When it comes to the idea of love, we're "all in," but we recoil at the thought of being held accountable for our actions. What's sad is that we often get stuck on this point of (mis)understanding, and we end up quitting on God, short-circuiting our quest to find Him. If we truly want to understand the reason for judgment, we must walk with Jesus Christ *all the way to the cross*, where He took upon Himself God's judgment of *our* sins, our moral failures. If one day you find yourself standing at this crossroad, please do not turn back and give up looking for the truth. At the cross, the Judge has taken off His robe, stood in your place for sentencing, and taken upon Himself the penalty for your sins. The only thing keeping us from knowing God, then, is our unwillingness to recognize what He has done for us.

I say this to preserve our dignity and self-esteem, because nothing could possibly be more humiliating than passing out of this life into eternity, only to find out that we quit the race one step from crossing the finish line.

More than once during my stay in Slovakia, I wanted to quit and just go home, but deep down I knew the Lord would carry me through it even though I was at my weakest point in my devotion to Him. Amazingly, God was still giving me opportunities to tell others about Him even though I was struggling within myself. My frailty did not mean that God was not there and moving in my life. He picked up the slack for me, and I believe my calling, however brief, was fulfilled. The entire school year afforded me a bird's-eye view of the extent of the Lord's love for me. He demonstrated His extreme faithfulness to me—and to His own purposes—because I was not bringing much to the table other than a willingness to participate when the opportunities to talk about Him popped up. Psalm 34:8 says:

> O taste and see that the Lord is good; how blessed is the man who takes refuge in Him!

Frankly, I wasn't even doing a very good job of taking "refuge" in Him, but I still saw the goodness of the Lord as He carried me through this year of testing.

Be cognizant, then, of God's proclivity for displaying His power *through **your** weakness*. If you look carefully at the Apostle Paul's life, you will see that he spent much of his adult life in a position of "weakness." He was beset by a problem described in 2 Corinthians 12:1-10 as a "thorn in the flesh," presumably a physical or spiritual affliction. He was not charismatic, nor was he a gifted public speaker, as you can glean from his description of the general opinion people held of his oratory gifts in 2 Corinthians 10:10:

> For they say, "His letters are weighty and strong, but his personal presence is unimpressive and his speech contemptible."

And, yes, some of his "letters," which make up a portion of the New Testament, were written from a Roman prison, or at least during a time of captivity. In his second letter to the church at Corinth, he wrote this:

> And He has said to me, "**My grace is sufficient for you, for power is perfected in weakness**." Most gladly, therefore, I will rather boast about my weakness, so that the power of Christ may dwell in me. (2 Corinthians 12:9)

Paul's one abiding quality that sustained him through this process of abandoning self-interest was his sense of indebtedness to God. He called himself a "bond servant" of

Christ Jesus on more than one occasion. A bondservant is one who takes no wages, who willingly forfeits all rights to himself or herself for the sake of one's master. The foundation of this mindset is a deep love for God, leading to the "crucifixion" of *self*, the laying down of one's life (John 15:13) for another greater than himself:

> I [Paul] have been crucified with Christ; and it is no longer I who live, but Christ lives in me; and the life I now live in the flesh I live by faith in the Son of God, who loved me and delivered Himself up for me. (Galatians 2:20)

No one explains this process of being "crucified with Christ" better than Oswald Chambers. Please consider his description of how this verse becomes a reality in your life:

> These words mean the breaking and collapse of my independence brought about by my own hands, and the surrendering of my life to the supremacy of the Lord Jesus. No one can do this for me, I must do it myself. God may bring me up to this point three hundred and sixty-five times a year, but He cannot push me through it. It means breaking the hard outer layer of my individual independence from God, and the liberating of myself and my nature into oneness with Him; not following my own ideas, but choosing absolute loyalty to Jesus. Once I am at that point, there is no possibility of misunderstanding. Very few of us know anything about loyalty to Christ or understand what He meant when He said, "...**for My sake**" (Matthew 5:11). That is what makes a strong saint.[11]

Hopefully, as you walk with God, you will come to this point of identification and exchange with Him. We must not fight against this God-ordained surrender of our souls. It is this supernatural course of events that God prescribes for our lives, this exchange of our "life" for His will. We must allow Him to have His way with our hearts. John the Baptist evinced his understanding of this principle when, after hearing that Jesus was beginning to baptize people, said this in John 3:30:

> **"He must increase, but I must decrease."**

Part of this process, this exchanging of our lives for God's plan, also takes place as we work our way through life's challenges and problems. Difficulty is coming to all of us, but the key is our attitude and response to the inevitable:

> In this you greatly rejoice, even though now for a little while, if necessary, you have been distressed by various trials, so that the proof of your faith, being more precious than gold which is perishable, even though tested by fire, may be found to result in praise and glory and honor at the revelation of Jesus Christ. (1 Peter 1:6-7)

Fortunately, God loves us and will aid us in the process of accepting His will and our circumstances, however difficult that process may be. My first short-term mission trip to Guatemala brought me face up with this rite of passage. My church was financing a school in the town of Cantel, which is in the western, mountainous region near Quetzaltenango, the largest city in western Guatemala. We purchased the facility and also paid the principal's and teachers' salaries. Once a year we took a group down there to do a Vacation Bible School for the kids and whatever other projects—building or otherwise—that might be needed.

On our second night there, we were on our way back to our hotel on the dimly lit highway running between Cantel and Quetzaltenango. As we overshot the left turn we needed to make off the highway, our driver braked to bring us to a skidding halt. Unfortunately, a large, Greyhound-like bus was directly behind us and could not stop in time to avoid hitting the rear of the van hard enough to spin us around. I was sitting in the left corner of the rearmost seat, which absorbed the brunt of the impact.

The next thing I knew, I awoke, as if from a long, bad dream, to see all three of us in the rearmost seat slumped over the back of the seat in front of us. It took us a minute or so to even realize what had happened before we could raise ourselves up and exit the van. I was bleeding from the scalp and face, as were several other people. I staggered around the crash site, trying to figure out what had happened. I must have looked pretty bad because someone in our group told me to go lie down on the side of the road until help arrived.

One woman in our van was ejected from the vehicle through a window, so violent was the impact. She lost some teeth and had other injuries. They eventually decided to load us in a car and head for the nearest hospital. I remember trying to comfort Patti, who was in significant pain, and someone telling me not to touch her because she was bleeding so badly. When we arrived at the hospital, there were enough of us hurt that they went into a sort of "triage" mode for a few hours. I was experiencing tremendous pain, but it was some time before the doctors got to me. I remember lying there muttering to myself, "Too much pain, too much pain." I think I asked for morphine.

My next conscious memory occurred about two-and-a-half days later, a condition apparently resulting from being heavily sedated. It's an eerie feeling to basically "lose" two days of your life and have no conscious memory of that time span. The doctors then told me I had suffered a spinal subluxation, which is what happens when one or more of the bones in your spine has moved out of its proper position in relation to the rest of the spine. I would need to be moved to a hospital in Guatemala City for surgery, they said. Mentally, I was pretty fuzzy at this point, so every detail of what I was being told didn't exactly register with me. I was so grateful to find out that one of the women in our group, Janie, was a nurse, and she took it upon herself to stay with me through this whole time. She even called my parents to let them know what had happened.

After a long ride down the mountain highway, I found

myself back in Guatemala City where the trip had started. Only this time I was at a private hospital, Herrera Llerandi, instead of the comfy confines of the Hotel Pan American. At this point, Janie contacted my parents and gave them the news. My dad and my brother Brian both decided to board a plane and come down, which definitely lifted my spirits. By the time they arrived, the doctors had already put me in cervical traction, a distinctly unpleasant experience. They inserted the two pointed prongs of a triangular-shaped metal rod into the opposite sides of my skull and then attached a weight to the top of the bar (the apex of the triangle), and the weight hung over an elevated bar behind my head. This was designed to "pull" the spine apart, providing the opportunity for muscles to relax and pinched nerves to be released. It was an acutely uncomfortable experience, one not recommended for the casual vacationer.

Lying in a hospital bed gives one time to think, and the irony of my situation was beginning to dawn on me. I had embarked on this trip with high hopes of sharing Christ with people and helping them know His salvation, but here I was flat on my back and out of commission for the foreseeable future. About this time, the rest of the group showed up to visit me, and it was then that I found out that Mark, who was driving the van the night of the wreck, had been detained by the local authorities. Apparently, Guatemalan law at that time mandated only two options for any driver involved in an automobile accident in which injuries occur. Either the driver goes to the hospital, or they are held in custody pending a possible trial should there be any charges filed by the authorities or the parties involved in the accident. I had to sign a waiver/release stating I would not press charges or sue because of my injuries in order for them to release Mark from custody.

My dad told me they were going to take a piece of bone

from my hip to fuse the fifth and sixth vertebrae in my neck together, thereby preventing further movement of the spinal column, which was fine by me. My surgeon, Dr. Sosa, was a believer, too, and he prayed with my dad before the surgery. He told Dad something to the effect that "we've already had two miracles because he wasn't paralyzed in the accident, and he wasn't injured during the bumpy ambulance ride from the mountains back down to Guatemala City. At this point, we need to ask God for a third miracle: to guide my hands during the surgery." I came though the surgery completely fine, and they put me in a contraption that was a combination neck and head brace, different but similar in function to the "halos" they use now. I wore this 24/7. Not only was sleep rendered virtually impossible by this device, but my doctors also told me I needed to stand and walk in a completely erect position, like a soldier at attention, or else my spine would heal improperly and permanently ruin my posture.

The two weeks spent in the hospital recovering were on the boring side. Fortunately, two ladies from my home church who were on staff with Youth With A Mission (YWAM) in Guatemala City—Laura and Tracy—volunteered to chauffeur my dad around town and bring him to the hospital for visits. Those visits were the highlight of my day. They got quite a kick out of my dad and his old-school ways. I think the only food they found to his liking there was Pollo Campero, the chicken shack franchise. My brother made his own way around town and came by every day, sometimes by himself and sometimes with Dad.

I was disappointed when the doctor told me I would not be able to return home after leaving the hospital. Because the possible turbulence of a plane ride would have posed too much of a risk to my newly refurbished neck, I would need to stay in Guatemala for at least six to eight weeks, he said. A lady from the U.S. Embassy came to visit me, but she didn't offer any suggestions for a temporary home, so my dad talked with the YWAM people, and they agreed to put me up in their office compound, which was in Guatemala City.

After finally leaving the hospital, Dad and I holed up in his hotel for a week before he had to leave. The one moment I will never forget from this experience was the day he had to fly back home. I had never seen my Dad cry before, but he wept openly and told me this: "You will never know how much God loves us until you are a parent and your child is in danger." Unforgettable stuff, coming from my normally reticent father.

After Dad left, I moved into the YWAM office, and it proved to be the perfect arrangement. About seven or eight people worked out of the office, and I was able help them with various projects during my stay there. I visited some of the local schools for fun, and I in turn was visited by people God sent to encourage me. Stan and Gail Wick were with Wycliffe Bible Translators, and they came every week, as did Edgar, who had been the translator for our original group. Sadly, about a year later he would pass away, the victim of a mysterious stomach ailment. Tracy and Laura also came by frequently, so I had some visitors. All in all, I'd have to say the Lord took very good care of me.

I often wonder how I would have reacted had I been permanently injured in the accident. Since I suffered no permanent debilitation from the injury, it was easy to be thankful about it. I'm not sure I would have responded with that same attitude had I been paralyzed. There were other lasting reminders of this trip—my hip "buzzed" for many years after the surgery, which I regard as God's way of reminding me how capable He is of taking care of me. The scar running down the back of my neck has also triggered many retellings of these events.

On the surface, this event had no obvious purpose in my life other than teaching me to trust the Lord in adverse circumstances, but sometimes God uses your trials and struggles to influence other people. You never know who is watching as you go through these difficulties. Such was the case with my adventure in Guatemala. In fact, one of my co-workers at the time, Todd—a gentleman who would later become my boss—was indeed watching. While I was in Guatemala, he was dating a lady who had taken on the work normally done by my administrative assistant. She was communicating back and forth with me by letter and also sharing her Christian faith with Todd.

Many years after the accident, I was on a job interview and the guy doing the hiring turned out to be Todd! After the interview, he took me aside and told me that my ordeal in Guatemala, among other things, had influenced him to put his faith in Christ. At the time Guatemala was happening, I had no idea God was using the whole situation to affect someone else.

So, please understand that whatever you may be called to endure or suffer through as a Christian *is not only about you.*

At times, the Lord is using you as Exhibit A in the furtherance of His kingdom, and your faith in the midst of trials or difficult circumstances is being used as evidence to convince someone else of the reality of God. He is at work in the lives of others; they may need a living example to look to for inspiration and guidance.

As my wife Shirley is fond of quoting, "Sometimes you are the only Bible a person will ever read."

10
Is God Trustworthy?

IN SEARCHING FOR God, it's very easy to be derailed by our frame of reference. Maybe we had a poor relationship with our father, or we've been hurt by someone in a church setting. Our mindset about God could be a distant one. We see Him as "religion" or merely a "concept" or a "supreme being," or, worse, as someone who wants to take our fun away.

Is it possible He actually has a distinct personality? Is it possible His relationship goals are as pragmatic as our own: *we want to know and be known,* to be a significant part of someone else's life?

I believe God created us for the purpose of being in relationship with Him, and above all else, He wants to engage with us in an intimate and deeply satisfying friendship. Most religions do not offer anything in the form of relationship but instead cast their god(s) as transcendent, unknowable beings who merely dole out orders, expectations, and punishment as he/she/they see fit. Again, though, with the God of the Bible, we are not talking religion; we are talking *relationship.*

If we come at God strictly from the impersonal standpoint, i.e. He is nothing more than a rule maker, dispassionate judge, or harsh taskmaster, then we have totally misunderstood who He really is. Beware of thinking you can "conceptualize" who God is. We must have an actual encounter with Him to know Him. The exciting part is that it's not necessary to wait for some cataclysmic, life-altering event to occur before you seek Him out. *He is there now*, waiting for you to begin moving His direction. But, He will not force Himself on you. You have to want Him.

Once He sees you begin to move His direction, He, in turn, starts moving toward you, and, trust me: It *will* be a life-changing event when you finally meet the God who created the sun and moon and the heavens. You will have no doubt who it is you have just encountered because the joy He ignites in your heart will be like nothing you have ever experienced before.

As you begin moving toward God, you will be "saved" when you finally say "yes" in your heart to the Lord Jesus Christ. That experience can be vastly different for each one of us. For those of us who grew up in the church, it is often a gradual awakening; for those of us with no spiritual background, they may encounter the Lord in much more sudden fashion. It varies according to your specific personality, but rest assured, God knows you better than you know yourself, and if you are willing to listen and respond, He will reveal Himself to you in a manner perfectly suited to you and your circumstances. Psalm 139 should be required reading for all of us because therein our Lord establishes His authorship over our creation and our personality. Verse 16 says this:

> Your eyes have seen my unformed substance;
> And in Your book were all written
> The days that were ordained for me,
> When as yet there was not one of them.

In contrast to God's unlimited perspective on our lives, you and I are prisoners of the time-space continuum. We only understand life to the extent that we understand the past. The present and future are mysteries to us—the present because it is unfolding instantaneously before our eyes (you *Star Trek* fans already knew that) and the future for the obvious reason. Thankfully, God has no such limitations; He is *eternal*, and all of time and history—past, present, and future—is "framed" right there in front of Him, as if He was looking at all of it on a smartphone screen. Psalm 139 begins by stating exactly how intimately He knows us:

> O Lord, You have searched me and known me.
> You know when I sit down and when I rise up;
> You understand my thought from afar.
> You scrutinize my path and my lying down,
> And are intimately acquainted with all my ways.
> Even before there is a word on my tongue,
> Behold, O Lord, You know it all.
> You have enclosed me behind and before,
> And laid Your hand upon me.
> Such knowledge is too wonderful for me;
> It is too high, I cannot attain to it. (Psalm 139:1-6)

This psalm is the genesis of trust because God lays it all out right here. He knows our first and last breath. He made us. He knows what we are going to say, do, and think in our lifetime. If we meditate on this facet of God's character—His eternal-ness—hopefully, our response will be one of implicit trust in His ability to direct the course of our lives. Unfortunately, we like the idea of writing our own story. Too often we resemble the malcontent actor or actress who constantly wants to improvise and rewrite the script rather than let the director run the show. But that is a tricky balance, too, because life is replete with contradictions. Even when we are close to the Lord, we may become caught in the fallout of poor choices made by others that seem beyond our control. There's the real rub because if their choices result in us having to endure the consequences of their sin, that really grates against us.

I was in a Bible study once with a man whose wife divorced him after he became a Christian. She found his newfound faith vexing and intolerable. That's not so unusual in and of itself, but Gavin (not his real name) had left some Christian books behind after the divorce was final and he had moved out of the house. His ex-wife apparently began reading through his library, and she ended up giving her life to Christ as a direct result of those books.

I don't know about you, but that outcome would have prompted me to ask God some serious questions about His methods, had I lived through that scenario myself. We know God hates divorce, so why did Gavin have to lose his wife, only to see her find the Lord afterward? I'm not sure I could stand up under that paradox, but he did and eventually remarried.

Gavin was down in the fire, down in the crucible, but he trusted God through a seemingly implausible situation that had a very ironic, improbable outcome. All of us will eventually go through some experience where life seems to be contradicting God and asking us to endure circumstances that don't make a whole lot of sense, but we must stay the course and hold fast until God resolves our dilemma. You can't really pray or even prepare for this kind of experience, but *it is coming* at some point in your life.

Nowhere in the Bible is this principle more pronounced than in Abraham's offering of his son Isaac in Genesis 22. God specifically, without any explanation, instructed Abraham to offer his son as a burnt offering. On their way up Mount Moriah to prepare the offering, Isaac questioned his father, asking where the lamb was for the burnt offering. Abraham responded to him, "God will provide for Himself the lamb for the burnt offering, my son." Here we find Abraham demonstrating a deep knowledge of God's ability to come through in a tight situation. He didn't waver from his task. He bound Isaac to the wood and raised the knife to slay his son, but God stopped him dead in his tracks, saying,

> "Do not stretch out your hand against the lad, and do nothing to him; for now I know that you fear God, since you have not withheld your son, your only son, from Me." (Genesis 22:12)

Abraham was willing to risk his most precious possession—his son—on a mere word from God. You may one day encounter a similar "crisis" point in your life when you will simply have to take God at His word, despite how wrong something feels to you.

To be honest, you may feel like this at various times in your journey with the Lord. When I first encountered Him, I was so overwhelmed with joy that I wanted to learn everything I possibly could about Him. The first three years or so after this event were marked by excitement and discovery as I absorbed everything I was reading and hearing about cultivating a relationship with God. He healed me almost instantly of some long-standing sins and fears. Profanity disappeared from my vocabulary. For years I had been afraid of public speaking. Getting up in front of people was something I wouldn't do. I even took lower grades in high school because of this fear. Wouldn't you know it, one of the first things I did after Christ came into my life was to get up in front of about 100 people on Easter morning to tell them what had happened to me! My fear was gone, replaced by calm confidence.

Those first few years of excitement and discovery did not last indefinitely, though. I began to struggle with family, relationship, and work-related issues. It was as though I went through an "incubation" period when God built into my life the bedrock of our relationship and then said, "Alright, now, it's time to get to work on the rest of you." I began to discover that some of my relationship issues stemmed from my family environment, my long-strained relationship with my dad, and long-standing difficulties building and maintaining simple friendships. Relationships felt like work to me.

I knew my relationship with my dad needed much work. Actually, he was one of the first people to talk to me about

God. That event occurred in January 1981 after I had been arrested for drunk driving after a Super Bowl party. I spent about four hours that evening in a Kansas City, Missouri, jail cell—one of the most humbling experiences of my life. My brother Brian had to bail me out with money he had won at a party earlier in the evening. Prior to that I had been fired from my job at a drapery company, too, so having no income, I was in need of money to pay a lawyer to help me get the charges reduced. I asked my parents if I could return home to live with them, and they graciously said yes.

Upon returning home—in fact, upon walking through their front door—one thing was readily apparent: Their relationship had changed for the better. There was a sense of peace between them, and they were touching each other again. Something had definitely changed in my absence, and I was about to discover for myself the impetus behind their transformation.

After a few weeks there, my dad approached me one evening and asked me how I felt about God. I had no answer. He sat down with me in the kitchen and began by telling me he knew I was depressed, but there was hope. He gave me a book of Bible verses and, if I remember correctly, Norman Vincent Peale's well-known book, *The Power of Positive Thinking*.[12] He told me he would be praying for me to find a job soon. In about two weeks, I found one. In fact, I had two job offers, one part-time and one full-time, so I accepted both positions. One of the jobs turned out to be my first position in manufacturing, which would eventually become the arena where I would find my career niche in production and inventory management.

"Maybe there is something to this prayer thing," I thought. Peale's book didn't really hold my attention, but over the next few months, I began to read the book of Bible verses and pray

them back to God. Not being that familiar with praying, it was sort of a test run for me, and I began to see what I thought were answers to those prayers. They were simple prayers. I remember one I said for a good night's sleep, and I had an absolutely serene nap that evening.

Someone else then reentered the picture. I had made numerous attempts at contacting my good friend Pegi, who was with me the night I was arrested on my DUI charge. I finally got ahold of her, and she told me she had moved recently. She told me her new roommate was a "Christian," and then she let go with this shocker: "I've decided that being a Christian is the most important thing in my life."

"Whoa, hold on a second," I thought, "Why do you need to be a Christian? You're already the best person I know, so why would you need that?"

She later invited me to come to her church and hang out with some of the people there. I went on a few campouts with this group, and the people were very kind, albeit somewhat different from my usual group of friends, and it seemed they all had a story to tell about their experiences with God. Since I had no equivalent experience, I kept quiet and listened. I didn't understand everything they were talking about, but that was okay too. Their church services surprised me because they sang songs taken directly from biblical text (primarily the Psalms) as opposed to conventional songs written "about" God. Their overall kindness affected me deeply. They weren't throwing parties for me or doing anything dramatic to speak of, but at that point in my life, I perceived their kindness as love.

Bear this in mind when you are around nonbelievers. God can use the smallest, most simple acts of kindness to draw someone to Himself. Yes, people sometimes come to faith because of some cataclysmic event or epiphany in their lives, but just as often salvation is precipitated by a series of smaller "encounters" spread out over time—an accumulation of events God uses to gradually draw someone to His Son.

That December, Dad invited me to come to church with him. Why not, I thought, I don't have anything else going on this Sunday. As I sat through sermons and Sunday School for several weeks, the integrity of the Bible was what made an impact on me. It was concrete, and my life was not. I joined a men's Bible study shortly thereafter, and one evening we attended a revival at a Baptist church. Having only been in church for about three years (ages 8 -10), I wasn't well-schooled on exactly what occurred at a "revival." My parents watched Billy Graham crusades on TV when I was a kid, but I could never figure out what the reverend was yelling about.

Once we arrived, I took my seat, not knowing what to expect or how it worked. The man speaking was a Russian-born Jew who was also a Christian (a "Messianic" Jew). As he finished, he asked everyone to bow their heads for prayer. Praying in public was new to me, but I went along with it. I remember his words so well: "I want everyone here who wants to be with God to raise their hand," he exclaimed. I thought he was asking for a consensus vote—a roll call. All these church people were going to raise their hands, right? I enthusiastically shot up my hand and then waited. Silence... followed by still more silence. I became a little nervous because everybody was dead quiet, not a sound anywhere. Then I heard this booming voice: "Alright, young man, I want you to get up out of your seat and come up here to receive Jesus Christ as your Lord and Savior."

Young *man?* I sat there frozen, completely stunned, with my hand still up, and then broke out into a cold sweat as I realized that, yes, I was the **only** person among all these people (200-strong, mind you) with my hand up. He had singled me out in that crowd. Bear in mind how petrified I was about getting up in front of people anyway, and here I was, trapped, with no way out. Had God tricked me into raising my hand? I started physically shaking as I tried to gather enough courage to lift myself out of that church pew. Getting up felt like I was trying to pull an oak tree out of the ground. Despite the nauseating fear, I managed to make my way out of the pew, squeezing through in front of all the guys I came with from my Bible study. *"Now all of these guys in the Bible study will know I'm not a Christian,"* I thought, groaning meekly to myself.

My cover was blown.

My surprise quickly turned into outright embarrassment because I knew there was no turning back now. I had to go through with it or else leave there feeling like a certified wimp. I made my way up the center aisle, where an exceedingly polite man approached me and invited me to go backstage with him to talk about Jesus. He started telling me what I needed to do. Unfortunately, I can't recall most of what he said because I was so traumatized and shell-shocked by the surprise of being singled out and put "on stage" that I was in a muddled daze. He prayed with me and asked me how I felt. "I feel like a weight has been lifted off my shoulders," I said. But I was lying. I really felt disoriented and kind of in shock, like one feels after emerging from a car wreck. I was only saying what I thought you were *supposed* to say. My goal was to get out of there so I could go home and try to put myself back together.

I was in a zombie-like trance riding home. I had no real idea what I had just done or what, if anything, would happen as a result of it. Paul, our Bible study sponsor and leader, pulled me aside as we got out of the car and told me I could call him if I had any questions. Are you kidding me? I had nothing *but* questions because the whole experience completely freaked me out. Little did I know, my life was about to take another very bizarre turn.

Fast-forward to the next morning. I got up and went to work, sat down to start, and I felt really strange in my abdominal area. It felt like I had something about the size of a baseball lodged in there. This was beyond weird. I knew I was a little traumatized by the events of the previous night, but this was really too much. This sensation lasted all day, and I went home, still feeling this alien entity in my stomach. It was very definitely there even if I couldn't explain it. Next morning, off to work. Same discomfort. At this point, I began to panic because *this was not my imagination*; there was really something that felt like a baseball inside of me. I knew what an upset stomach felt like; I knew what nervous butterflies felt like; this was *way* beyond that.

Remembering Paul's offer, I called him, told him I needed to talk, and basically invited myself to dinner the following night. I was feeling pretty desperate. This was an intense, out-of-control, freaked-out situation, and I didn't know what else to do. I said nothing about the baseball; I knew he'd think I was crazy.

What happened next was completely unexpected.

The next morning I went to work. The baseball was gone! *Instead of anxiety, my heart—in fact, my whole being—was flooded with the most intense, all-consuming **joy** I had ever experienced in my entire life!* I felt like a volcano was erupting inside of me! No drug I had ever used could even *begin* to approach the explosive joy being ignited in my heart on this day. I was glad no one else was in the office that morning because I could not focus on my work. I paced around the room reciting John 3:16 multiple times:

> For God so loved the world that He gave His only begotten son, that whoever believes in Him shall not perish, but have eternal life.

When had I learned that verse? Had I memorized it as a child? I didn't know, but I couldn't stop repeating it. I didn't totally understand how this was happening, but I knew this for sure: *My life had changed, and it was never going to be the same*—such was the intensity and power of God's presence! I knew then that the Lord was in my life and this incredible, electrical joy was His way of demonstrating that reality to me. The anxiety and confusion of the previous two days had turned into the most miraculous day of my life. Only the *real* God could flip reality on its head that quickly! I would later learn that this is what it felt like to be "born again" (John 3:3), to be filled with God's Spirit, the Holy Spirit.

After work, I went over to see Paul. I was still bouncing off the walls with my newfound joy, so I think he was taken aback by my sudden turnaround from the previous day's distress call. He had to talk me down so we could have a normal conversation. He realized that I had met the Lord, and he explained to me that even as a believer I would have some "mountaintop" days similar to this one and some days that felt more like I was "down in the valley." That calmed me down a little, but I was still flying when I left. I never told him about the baseball.

Paul was right. There would indeed be some days down in the "valley." In fact, there were many days down there. What I gradually discovered was that while the Lord removed some sins from my life right away, such as profanity, there were many temptations He left for me to work through too. As I delved further into the Bible, it became apparent this was normal. People had "stuff" they had to deal with, mistakes they had to make amends for, and relationship issues they had to work on.

Very soon after my encounter with Christ, God had me up in front of about 100 people, bright and early on Easter morning, telling them about this experience. My dad stood in the middle of the crowd and directly in front of me. We made eye contact through much of my talk. I believe he was extremely proud of me, and our relationship began to heal that day. This event also marked the first time I had ever stood up to speak before a large group of people without dreading the experience. That nauseating, crippling fear was gone.

My brother Brian also noticed the change in me almost immediately. He came into my room one day and remarked how "different" I seemed to be acting. I told him that I had accepted the Lord, which he was thrilled to hear. I would later find out that Brian had been faithfully praying for me for a long time. In fact, Paul told me that when Brian was in high school, he prayed for me, without fail, at every Wednesday night youth group meeting. So, yes, God does hear our prayers!

A Word to Parents

Several months later, I attended a church concert where the singer was talking about his father and the ups and downs of their relationship. He ended by telling us to "go tell your dad you love him." I knew I needed to do that. A few nights later, I happened to be at my folks' house for dinner, and Dad and I sat down in the living room together to talk about God. I told him I loved him. He told me he loved me. I'm not sure I had ever heard those words come out of his mouth, so you can imagine how good that made me feel. We embraced after that. It was if God had orchestrated the whole evening. It was perfect.

I must add one crucial point about by my dad. We had a very distant, strained relationship during my teenage years and on into my early twenties, but he was there in my time of crisis, which is when I needed him the most. If you aspire to be a good father, a good parent, then take his example to heart. At some point in your child's life, there will likely arise a point of crisis, a point where this child will need someone to speak into his or her life the wisdom of God. When that event occurs, what you learned at work or on the street is not going to cut it. Your child is going to need *godly* wisdom, the kind that only comes from a power greater than ourselves. This is wisdom gleaned only from time spent in the crucible of life with God: trusting Him and learning from Him in difficult times. This wisdom has the power to alter the course of your son's or daughter's future. You don't want to fail your child when this event occurs; you want to be ready, which is all the more reason to diligently pursue your own relationship with the Lord.

Our children will discover in due time that determining God's will for their lives often takes a circuitous route as opposed to a straight line. Life is messy, unfortunately, and since kids are prone to take a few missteps of their own, our presence in their lives can significantly shorten the time it often takes to realign themselves with God's will. The less time they spend wandering in their own personal wilderness the better. But what happens if we are not there, not ready? The devil then has an opportunity to supplant the wisdom we could have supplied with someone else's voice or influence, which is seldom ever the *best* situation, since no one knows your kids as well as you do.

In addition to being there at their crisis point, we will need to bathe them in prayer because they don't know what they don't know, right? This is especially the case if they have no active relationship with the Lord, but even if they do, keep pleading their case before the Lord.

As their parent, we have a unique vantage point, one that

is acutely aware of their deepest needs. No one else can supply the prayers that we can on their behalf.

11
HOW DO WE KNOW GOD LOVES US?

MORE HAS BEEN written about it than any other subject. It's been misused, abused, and distorted so often. Love. It's the answer to all of our problems—or the source of them, depending on your perspective at the moment. Of the four Greek words in the Bible that are translated into English as the expression "love," the one that most accurately describes God's love is "agape." The Dutch author Bas Heijne has described it thus:

> "Agape is the concrete commitment to the flourishing of someone or something outside of oneself. Even and perhaps especially when that flourishing, hence the joy, is threatened."[13]

God's specific goal is that each of us may be "conformed to the image of Christ" (Romans 8:29), and His love—agape love—revolves around that process. Much like a potter shapes and molds clay as it spins on his pottery wheel, God's chief aim is to make us more like His Son Jesus. Part of the process involves what I like to call "real love." The Lord has a way of applying gentle pressure in areas where we have "stuff" going on in an attempt to encourage us to deal with our issues. He may even allow us to have difficult experiences that will hopefully produce lasting changes in our lives. As Proverbs 17:3 so perfectly states:

> The refining pot is for silver and the furnace for gold, but the Lord tests hearts.

What is the testing process being spoken of here? We know that some metals are refined by burning away the dross: the impure substances that surround them. Does God allow us to be tested in much the same way? He certainly allowed Job to be tested, permitting Satan access and free reign in Job's life for a fairly extended period of time. But as a result, Job gained a deeper understanding of who God was, learning in the process that what he suffered was not irredeemably painful, but instead resulted in a wiser, even more compassionate Job.

At the peak of his suffering, Job's friends gave him some cruel, wrong-headed counsel and advice, but Job did not hold them in contempt; instead, he prayed for them, and God then restored his fortune and family to an even greater degree than existed before the calamity. They were friends behaving like enemies, but Job learned to love his very unlovable "friends." This is one of the primary character traits God will attempt to build into your life, one that will take a great deal of cooperation on your part and one that may require you to consume large quantities of humble pie along the way:

> "You have heard that it was said, 'YOU SHALL LOVE YOUR NEIGHBOR and hate your enemy.' "But I say to you, **love your enemies** and pray for those who persecute you, so that you may be sons of your Father who is in heaven; for He causes His sun to rise on the evil and the good, and sends rain on the righteous and the unrighteous." (Matthew 5:43-45)

You can't prepare in advance for this experience. It's more like on-the-job training. Learning to endure and bear the sins of others is the ultimate character test. God is testing your heart in this way by allowing you to see exactly what is in it, be it hatred, jealousy, or, hopefully, love. As part of this process, you will find He wants to move you *toward* your "enemies" rather than away from them. As much as you might be offended by their behavior, God loves them with the same passion with which He loves you. God goes after the bad egg, the black sheep, and the wayward son—even your enemy. No creature can go unloved, and there is no creature hidden from His sight (Hebrews 4:13).

This is one of the most useful lessons we have to learn as believers. God expects us to pursue peace even when we are mistreated or feel that something unjust or unfair has occurred. He will aid us in developing this character trait by allowing us to experience some of these situations, so don't be surprised if you encounter what seems to be unfair treatment on multiple occasions. God gives us very specific instructions on how we are to handle these situations:

> Never pay back evil for evil to anyone. Respect what is right in the sight of all men. If possible, so far as it depends on you, be at peace with all men. Never take your own revenge, beloved, but leave room for the wrath of God, for it is written, "VENGEANCE IS MINE, I WILL REPAY," says the Lord. "BUT IF YOUR ENEMY IS HUNGRY, FEED HIM, AND IF HE IS THIRSTY, GIVE HIM A DRINK; FOR IN SO DOING YOU WILL HEAP BURNING COALS ON HIS HEAD." Do not be overcome by evil, but overcome evil with good. (Romans 12:17-21)

Some years ago, a close friend of mine, Jack, was working for an organization that made small household appliances (toaster ovens, blenders, and things of that sort). One fellow he worked with (Ian) was initially his coworker but then became the head of Jack's department. Jack thought their relationship as coworkers had been amiable for the most part, but he later came to realize that his coworker had been unhappy with some of his work practices. They shared a common faith in God, and Jack had assumed all was well before this illusion was shattered by the events described below.

The story began fairly innocently and involved the people who worked on one of the assembly lines in the manufacturing plant. Their supervisor had vacated his position, and Ian was looking for someone to step into that role. Jack was almost sure he would be offered the position because he was the production planner responsible for the various electric fans produced on that line. Since he set the schedule for each day's work on the line, he was directly responsible for assigning these people a very substantial portion of their workload. He interacted with them virtually every day.

His assumption turned out to be correct. Jack's first question for Ian when he offered him the job was: "How much more money will that mean for me?" He would have been taking on five to six more people in addition to the one he was currently supervising, so naturally he thought that would at least mean a raise, if not a promotion, too. He was overdue on the raise anyway.

How wrong Jack was. Ian told him there would not be any more money, nor would this be considered a promotion; it was simply additional responsibility. In fact, he was told he could either accept the job as offered or take 30 days to find another one. At this point, Jack thought about raising a ruckus with management over the issue of the non-raise and the "forced" termination, but he decided to sit on the decision for a few days. He really felt the ultimatum was unfair, but he didn't protest. Early the next week, he declined the offer and told Ian he would begin looking for another position. Ian accepted Jack's "resignation."

Shortly thereafter, Jack attended a Christian retreat where the main speaker happened to be a local pastor. One evening, he had each person come up so he could pray for them individually and also to see if God might have a specific word to speak to them. When Jack came up to the podium, the pastor looked at him, paused for a moment, and said this:

"God wants you to know…that He knows the one who has taken away your authority."

That was it; that was all he said. Jack turned and went back to his seat.

In his spirit, Jack immediately sensed that the word of knowledge shared with him could only be about one thing. The *only* place where he held a position of "authority" was at work, and it was starkly obvious to Jack that the Lord was addressing the situation with his boss, the job, and accompanying raise that, logically speaking, Jack thought should have been his. Upon recovering from the startling realization that God had spoken directly to him through another person, he left the meeting with this thought:

"Wow, Lord, if You've got this, I'm not going to touch it; I'll just stand back and let You do Your thing and see what happens."

Happen it did! The company was struggling to make a profit, so management brought in a consultant to review the whole operation, top to bottom. One of the areas reviewed was production scheduling, which meant the spotlight was trained on Jack's boss Ian since he headed up that aspect of the operation. The consultants started quizzing him about the nuts and bolts of production, finally getting around to who did the scheduling and what exactly this person was responsible for both system-wise and people-wise. He proceeded to describe Jack's job, and he happened to mention that he was leaving soon.

They then asked Ian if he was familiar with some of the technical aspects of scheduling and whether or not he could execute Jack's responsibilities in his absence. After hearing Ian's response, the consultants became concerned about replacing Jack. They were fairly adamant and insisted that Jack remain employed at least a couple months until Ian could find someone with the knowledge base and skills to fill Jack's shoes. When the meeting was over, Ian pulled Jack aside and asked him if he would stay a few months longer. Jack responded, "Sure, just change my status from a 'termination' to a 'lay off.'" His boss agreed. So, Jack went from a situation where he felt like he was being forced out to one where he was, in a sense, restored to his rightful standing in the company, if only temporarily. Did the Lord engineer this circumstance? You can guess how Jack felt.

Jack remained there a couple months and then hit the streets to find another job. Soon after leaving, he called one of the vice presidents who had been a mentor to him there and discovered that Ian had left the company only a few weeks after he did. His mentor said something to the effect that Ian had been "out to get him" and that he had been unhappy with Jack long before the aforementioned incident occurred. Looking back on it, Jack's best guess was that his boss had never liked his methods of assigning work to the fan line personnel when they were coworkers.

The story does not end there. Turn the page forward about 10 years later in time. One afternoon after work, Jack had decided to stop by a post office to mail a care package to a friend living overseas. A minivan, full of people and packed to the gills with all manner of luggage and clothes, pulled up next to him. To Jack, it looked like a major family vacation was in progress.

As Jack started toward the post office door, who do you suppose emerged from the driver's seat of the van? He didn't recognize his former boss at first, but Ian recognized Jack right away, though he seemed to have forgotten his name. He asked Jack how he had been and told him he had often wondered what became of him. Jack in turn asked him what he had been up to, and Ian replied that he had been doing maintenance work for a local school district for the past seven years. Now, after all this time, he had finally found a much more lucrative job in manufacturing, and he and the family were on their way to their new out-of-state home that very day! The whole meeting was surreal, Jack said, with the conversation lasting only a few minutes; then his boss was gone.

Looking back on it, Jack said he often wondered if the whole scenario could have been avoided had he recognized how badly he had offended his boss when they were coworkers. At any rate, he was thankful that the Lord disclosed to him at the retreat His foreknowledge of the situation, because that made it far easier to trust God for the eventual outcome.

Trusting the Lord in the midst of these adverse situations is important, not only for our sake, but also for the sake of those who are—*trust me*—watching us to see how we handle the trial. Our behavior will either be useful to God as He works to draw people to Christ—or not. Fortunately, He does not tire of repeating this lesson for us if we fail to grasp its significance for others who may not know Him yet.

In terms of biblical examples, Jonah would be a prime example of someone who had to step up to the task and learn the art of forbearance before he could fulfill God's purpose in his life. Jonah was in the belly of the whale three days and three nights, which is the story we may have learned as kids. But the important part of the story is how he got there.

God had asked Jonah to go and preach repentance to the Ninevites, who were a barbaric, ruthless people Jonah hated with a passion. He refused to go. In his judgment, the Ninevites were not worthy of God's forgiveness, so he defied God's wishes and instead stowed away at sea on a ship. Sound familiar? Like Adam and Eve before him, he attempted to "hide" from God, which, of course, was folly. God caused raging storms and calamity to befall the sailors on the ship. To their credit, they recognized that the hand of God was against them, and they rightly perceived they were travelling with someone who was at odds with the Lord. When Jonah finally confessed, the sailors threw him overboard where he was swallowed by the whale, the action of which simultaneously stopped the storms. Not until he relented and acknowledged God's lordship over his life was Jonah released from his dark, watery prison. God then repeated His directive to go and preach to the Ninevites, and this time Jonah acceded to His request. The Ninevites repented upon hearing Jonah's message, and their city was saved from the wrath of God.

We often suffer from the same malady as Jonah did. Our first response when confronted with evil is to be revolted by it, then to condemn it, and then to pronounce judgment in our hearts; however, the believer cannot pass judgment on the sins of others. We cannot hold on to bitterness or anger in our hearts and allow the offending party to become "indebted" to us. We cannot let bitterness hibernate in our hearts or in our minds. This is one of the hardest works the believer is called to because nothing is more difficult than loving the one who has inflicted pain upon you or a person you care about. Our hearts cry out for justice, but instead we must suspend our own judgment, which leaves space for the Holy Spirit to gain access to the perpetrator's heart.

When our judgment is taken out of the way, one of the Holy Spirit's primary impediments to changing our enemy's heart is removed. If, when confronted with his or her own sin, the offender meets *our* anger and ire, those emotions (and the response to them) will block him or her from experiencing the work of God's Spirit. The person in question will end up responding to us rather than to God. If, however, our "enemies" receive kindness from us despite not having deserved or earned it, our judgment is taken out of the way. The Lord then has a clear path to deal with their conscience as He goes about the work of having them reexamine their motives and actions. This can only happen when they receive love and mercy instead of retribution and a blessing instead of the angry, vengeful response they were expecting.

I have often heard people cite the opinion that while we are called to love others and forgive them, we are not to be used as "doormats." Obviously, in cases where abuse is involved, common sense dictates that we should remove ourselves from that environment. But when I address the believer's calling to love our enemies and suspend judgment, I am talking about the interaction that takes place in the normal course of living and working with others.

At times, we *will* feel like a "doormat" as a result of that interaction, but the trick is to immediately respond in love. Love may take the form of confronting the other person's actions (in a winsome way), or it may require us to return good for evil. It may even have us stand there in the fire taking whatever they are dishing out. This experience, while painful and (on the surface) humiliating, can still be used by God to strike a powerful blow for love. I have had people verbally accost me in a degrading and abusive fashion and then witness God do a mighty work as they later came back to me to ask for forgiveness. Likewise, I have been on the other side of the equation, wounding others with my tongue and having to go back to them to ask their forgiveness.

The primary advantage the believer has over the nonbeliever in coping with these situations is the presence of the Holy Spirit in our lives. While nonbelievers are often enslaved to their personal whims or emotions, we have a Helper (John 14:26), one who comes alongside us and is always pushing us toward restraint, reconciliation, and, if needed, repentance. Almost all of our important relationships have *some* degree of conflict we are required to manage, and that process can be difficult even with God's supernatural aid. Our marriage, family, and work relationships form the bedrock of our lives, so we need to make sure we are allowing the Holy Spirit to guide us through the inevitably thorny issues we will encounter in these arenas.

I remember one instance at work where I failed to resolve several inventory issues in a timely enough fashion for a very good customer of ours. My tardiness caused her to be tardy in responding to her customers, and they had let her know how unhappy they were about it. She sent me one of those emails full of thinly veiled anger that nevertheless evinced a profound dissatisfaction with my performance. You know the kind I'm talking about: the one you initially write to verbally undress a person when they make you unhappy but you think better of sending it to them in the end. Well, she went ahead and sent this one.

My initial response was anger as I mentally rehearsed my reply, which consisted of a litany of her own offenses and shortcomings in her role as a distributor representing my company. Fortunately, I took a deep breath first, and instead, I composed an email in which I first acknowledged my mistakes and then explained exactly why my responses were delayed. I took responsibility for and addressed the issues rather than her anger. My intention was to *"bless those who curse you, pray for those who mistreat you,"* as we are admonished to do in Luke 6:28. I figured it was best to first own it and then explain it.

She responded by calling me to thank me for being such a "good person, such an easy person to work with." Apparently, my email response totally disarmed her. She was extremely complimentary to say the least, and grateful, I think, that I did not respond in anger. Knowing her as I did, I suspect she regretted sending the email the instant after she pressed the SEND button, and I'll bet she was hoping it would not provoke a hostile reaction on my part.

For me, it was an edifying experience because God does

His mightiest work through very ordinary, seemingly insignificant encounters like this one. The devil (the real devil, Satan, not the horned cartoon character) was trying to create enmity between Sara and me. He was seeking to permanently rupture our relationship, but instead we gained a newfound respect for each other, and our friendship deepened because we stepped out of the judgment seat and made way for God to do that which He wanted to do in our hearts.

Is God a "mean" god then, asking us to embrace bad people and their bad behavior? No, He is loving. It's just that He can be somewhat… well… relentless… in loving us so completely and thoroughly. When Jesus adjures us to love our enemies, He is not making an idle suggestion. He is laying down the objective, giving us our marching orders on how to live life and how to regard people. Nothing is more important to Him than His lost sheep (the "unrighteous"), those whom He loves, and He is telling us that finding those sheep is worth everything and anything we might have to spend along the way to achieve that goal, including our dignity:

> "But I say to you, do not resist an evil person; but whoever slaps you on your right cheek, turn the other to him also. If anyone wants to sue you and take your shirt, let him have your coat also. Whoever forces you to go one mile, go with him two." (Matthew 5:39-41)

Unfortunately, those of us who have already been found by our Shepherd tend to have short memories. How easy it is to forget that we ourselves were once unrighteous and evil, lost sheep without hope in this life. Someone once treated us kindly when we were being a jerk; someone once was willing to go the extra mile with us, regardless of how irritating or ungrateful we acted; someone once helped us when we didn't necessarily deserve his or her efforts on our behalf; someone once ignored our proud, even arrogant, indifference to the truth and kept entreating us to find and follow Christ when that person should have left us to the futility of our own devices.

Christ will not let us settle for loving only those who treat us well. He demands we look beyond our precious pride and comfort. Not only that, He will touch every area of our lives, and He is not above pruning us to allow for new growth. Even the character qualities in ourselves we deem good may experience a makeover. He may also take some things out of our hands in order to position us better to hear and respond to Him. This can be a painful and even difficult process to understand because, as the rich young ruler in Mark 10:17-27 discovered, we have a tendency to grow attached to certain possessions (in his case, it was the property he owned) that can prevent us from responding to Christ when He is trying to enlist our cooperation.

To follow Christ is to be beholden to nothing in His place, that is, to make no throne in our hearts for any attitude or anything or anyone other than Him. If we fail this test (being willing to abandon whatever we are most fond of), then we will fail to discover the treasure that is "hidden" in Christ, and our lives will be but pale imitations of all that He intends for us to experience. An exchange needs to take place: our lives for the resurrected life He offers us. There can be no holding back on our part, no misplaced affection for people or items that will keep us from the Kingdom of God. We are meant to be reconcilers and ambassadors for Christ, and whatever hinders us from fulfilling that mission must be cast aside.

Moreover, we need to realize that God, our Father, has one very specific, over-arching goal in mind. He is trying to build **in us** the character of Jesus. What does that look like? It looks like a man who was the friend of the unseemly: prostitutes, tax collectors, dirt-poor widows. He loved those who were unlovable, including his enemies. He gave favor to those who didn't deserve it. Romans 8:29 might be one of the most important verses in the Bible because in it God states His overarching purpose for His children:

> For those whom He foreknew, He also predestined to become conformed to the image of His Son.... (Romans 8:29a)

The word in this passage is translated as "conformed," the Greek word *"summorphoo,"* or "to render like" or "to assimilate."[14]

God's chief work along this line begins with redeeming His creation and then continues nonstop as He works unflaggingly to free our character from whatever defects might obscure the display of His Son in and through us. This process never ends in this life. He is relentless to the point of testing us with fire. Our part is to not wilt or shrink back, to not give in to evil, but to pursue righteousness at any cost. Everything must be sacrificed if necessary because, as missionary Jim Elliot, hero of *Shadow of the Almighty* (a must-read), pointed out:

> **"He is no fool who gives what he cannot keep to gain that which he cannot lose."**[15]

Let those words sink into your soul, for whatever God builds into our lives, He builds into them for all eternity; therefore, whatever the cost, whatever we may have to give up to allow God to have His way in us is worth the expense to our souls, even if we must sacrifice our own agenda or pleasure.

To put it another way, the Lord is not interested in increasing our comfort level. He likes to keep us on our toes. Like any good trainer, He challenges us to grow, and, like it or not, we only grow when we are put amongst people and situations that stretch us. Have you ever noticed that in most groups of any size to which you belong, be it your workmates, circle of friends, church, or volleyball team, there exists that one person God has especially placed there to irritate you in the most annoying ways imaginable, while simultaneously wearing threadbare your patience? This person is part of God's plan. Learn to love him or her. God is using this person to shape your disposition: to make you more kind, compassionate, loving, merciful, and, yes, patient.

Have you ever noticed that all facets of your life are never perfectly in sync all at the same time? There is always some area that needs work, some thorn in your side that will not accommodate your efforts to avoid it. Learn to love the process of working it out. Dive in with your whole heart, and leave the results to God. Yes, this sounds like work and it may feel that way, but God is trying to mold you into a vessel useful for His purposes, so the process may be accompanied by some growing pains.

This refining, this shaping of character, His persistent attention to detail—this is the evidence of God's love for you. If your Christian life sometimes feels like you are walking through the fire, then rejoice, for God is at work in and through you.

I heard someone once describe his relationship with Christ by saying that "it hurts so bad it feels good." That doesn't sound like fun, you say, and you would be right, but would you rather God paid no attention to your character development at all? He is in the business of making us holy, and He loves us enough to allow us to go through some difficult experiences wherein we have to struggle and wrestle to pass through to the other side. Romans 5:3-5 puts it this way:

> And not only this, but we also exult in our **tribulations**, knowing that tribulation brings about **perseverance**; and perseverance, **proven character**; and proven character, **hope**; and hope does

not disappoint because the love of God has been poured out within our hearts through the Holy Spirit who was given to us.

Do you see the character development blueprint the Lord is working from here?

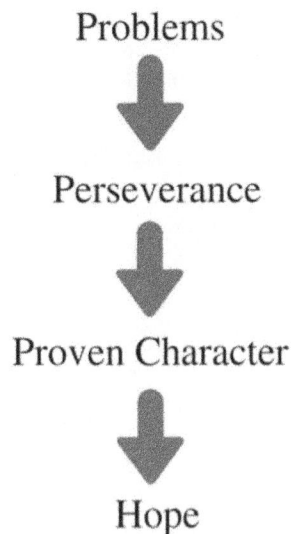

Hope is at the end of the continuum because that is the springboard for our life's work. If we have enough confidence in God's love for us to be willing to take chances, to be fearless, to allow Him to put us in a position of weakness so we can help other people, then we are useful to Him. He can trust us in even the most difficult and trying of situations. Do you know how good it feels to have God use you to make someone else's life better? There is nothing better in life than that feeling, to know that God has entrusted something or someone He loves to your care.

We sometimes groan and murmur because the people in our lives are so difficult to bear, but perhaps you are in that spot because God needs a person there He can count on, someone He can trust to endure even the most difficult and aggravating circumstances?

In Hebrews 12:11, we are reminded that God has a reward for those who persevere and do not shrink back from letting Him have His way in our lives:

> All discipline for the moment seems not to be joyful, but sorrowful; yet to those who have been trained by it, afterwards it yields the peaceful fruit of righteousness.

12
THEOLOGY AND A LITTLE DUST IN THE WIND

WHILE I APPRECIATE the need for sound theology based on biblical truth, I easily can become frustrated by people who use their theological "constructs" to put a box around God, so to speak. I'm wary of any attempt to circumscribe God's behavior because He alone determines how and when He will intervene in the course of history.

Recently, I participated in a group discussing the subject of whether or not God hears the prayers of non-Christians. One person pointed out that God only hears the "sinner's prayer" (a prayer of repentance) of a nonbeliever but does not hear any other type of prayer the person might offer. I understand the scriptural basis for that view, John 9:31 being the most obvious verse one might cite in support of this stance:

> We know that God does not hear sinners; but if anyone is God-fearing and does His will, He hears him.

Does that one verse completely preclude God hearing and regarding the prayers of the nonbeliever? In view of the sovereignty of God, I'm not sure we can limit God's action in the nonbeliever's life in any way. In my experience, even before I asked the Lord into my life, I offered prayers to God, and at the time I believed God was answering those prayers, even if they weren't specifically the "sinner's prayer."

That belief was part of what drew me to God and made me even hungrier to know more about Him. At the time, I did not know where my pursuit would lead me. My "concept" of

God was severely limited: It was merely an idea, one not informed by any real knowledge of God's character or person. I had no specific knowledge of who God was and how He was going to interact with me, and I wasn't certain that the God of the Bible was the one true God, although I know that now. I was looking for help, any kind of help, and meaning to my existence.

Who is to say there might not be many Muslims all over the world who are just as sincere as I was, just as hungry, and are offering prayers to a "god" (or their "concept" of God), but who are misguided or have been misdirected in looking to "Allah" as the one true God? Since they are praying to a false god, does that mean the one true God does not hear their prayers? Obviously God can hear anything and everything. The question then becomes: Does He respond to the seeking heart, irrespective of one's ignorance of Jesus Christ?

Before my encounter with Christ, I was praying to a god I did not "know." I was praying in ignorance, not knowing at that time exactly who or what I was looking for to fill up my emptiness. Even when I finally did ask Christ to come into my life, I didn't really comprehend the significance of what I was doing or what was going to happen afterwards. The outcome was a complete surprise to me. I would eventually come to understand exactly *how* it happened, but that, too, was a process.

I strongly identify with Kerry Livgren, founding member and chief songwriter for the progressive rock band Kansas, who spent years looking in the wrong places, exploring virtually every religion and syncretic philosophy he could get his hands on in his quest to find truth and meaning in his life. At one point, he thought he had found his answer in a massive tome called *The Urantia Book: Revealing the Mysteries of God, the Universe, World History, Jesus, and Ourselves*, which apparently espoused a synthesis of elements from many of the religions he had been investigating, including Christianity.[16] If the logic employed by my friends in the aforementioned discussion group were applied to Kerry's situation, one might deduce that any prayers or worship he may have been offering were probably not being heard, but that's not how the story ends.

Kerry eventually found Christ through a series of conversations with a fellow musician who gave him a copy of a book by Hal Lindsey, *The Liberation of Planet Earth*, which contained a very simple explanation of the gospel that prompted Kerry to surrender his life to Christ.[17] This series of events begs the following question: Was God not listening to Kerry all that time, until he happened to stumble upon the *correct* God? I think God honors the prayer of a sincere heart, and He eventually reached out and grabbed Kerry in the midst of his pursuit, which is what He did for me too. *He honored the **sincerity** of our search, misguided or ignorant as it was at times.*

The songs Livgren wrote for Kansas reveal a man who was searching the depths of his being—and the world's various "religions"—for the truth. I admire his unashamed spiritual hunger. Pick up almost any Kansas album recorded before he placed his faith in Christ and read the lyrics to his songs. You will encounter the ruminations of a man who was in profound pain, whose soul was in deep distress. He was on a mission: He was searching for the truth. He describes the human condition as alternating between the glimmering hope and promised peace of "Carry on Wayward Son" and the vivid, heartbreaking resignation of songs like "Dust in the Wind," where he laments the ephemeral, transitory nature of a life where nothing lasts, where nothing makes a difference in the end.[18]

It must have taken extraordinary courage to author words that so fully embrace the bleak futility of a life lived without God. He sounds overwhelmed by the immensity of life, comparing himself to a single raindrop falling into something as all-engulfing as the ocean. Here he confronts the most enervating, soul-crushing feeling of all: *insignificance*. All of this came from the heart of a man who had reached the pinnacle of his profession, having achieved rock star status with one of the most popular bands in the world at that time (mid-1970s to early 1980s). And what did he find?

Emptiness.

For those interested in finding out how Jesus Christ changed his despair into hope, Livgren's autobiography, *Seeds of Change* (also the title of his first solo recording) offers a fascinating chronicle of a man who went down more than a few rabbit trails in his quest to find God.[19] You can also find numerous video clips online where he recounts the events that led to his conversion.

As for theology, I take issue with people who say that God only works in a prescribed, particular way. They build their case out of scripture, but that case is still a contrived construct, engineered out of human thought, and therefore subject to possible limitations in human understanding. The Bible is definitely without error and is the unimpeachable Word of God, but I'm wary of those who use it to box God in…to limit Him in some way. Frankly, God is very capable of doing absolutely anything He wants to do.

Though the Bible is unquestionably sufficient revelation, I'm not sure we can call it exhaustive revelation. After all, God is still God, and He might do that which isn't specifically described in the Bible, such as "answer" a sincere prayer offered up in ignorance. He is not going to contradict His own nature or existing revelation in any way, but He is surely capable of more than we ascribe to Him—or at least more than we understand.

If we really believe in the concept of God's sovereignty, how can we place restraints upon God? I'm not suggesting in any way that we "add" anything to the contents of the Bible, His expressed will, but neither should we place limits on the actions of an all-loving, all-powerful God.

13
HOW TO DETERMINE GOD'S WILL FOR YOUR LIFE

DISCERNING GOD'S WILL in a given situation can be intimidating. Admittedly, it's not always a black-and-white process, and there are some gray areas in life that can require extra thought and prayer; however, I think God has some very conspicuous ways of revealing to us what direction to go in if we are looking to Him for guidance on a daily basis. His ideal for us is that we would be so closely linked to Him, like a branch is to the vine (John 15:1-3), that we would draw our very sustenance and nourishment for living from Him.

Doing His will should come as naturally as breathing. He wants us so close that *not* doing His will would be the exception, an aberration in our behavior. We are responsible for working out that relationship in prayer and for staying "tuned in" to how God speaks to us. God uses many different avenues to communicate with us. I have outlined some of them below.

The Bible

Definitely start with God's Word. Most of God's will regarding our moral and ethical choices can be found right here, and, above all else, if our actions are opposed to what God has explicitly stated, then we know we are not doing His will. Bringing our lives into line with God's will is a daily journey, so don't lose hope if you are struggling in some areas. Please read Micah 6:8 in the Old Testament; it provides a time-tested pattern for daily living:

> He has told you, O man, what is good;
> And what does the Lord require of you
> But to do justice, to love kindness,
> And to walk humbly with your God?

The Lord will sometimes speak directly to us through His Word, bringing a very specific verse or passage to our attention that gives us a frame of reference from which to proceed. Several years ago, I was asking God if I should go overseas to teach English as a second language. After a season of prayer and seeking counsel on the matter, I was sitting in church one morning reading through Joshua, and the Lord gave me Joshua 1:9:

> "Have I not commanded you? Be strong and courageous! Do not tremble or be dismayed, for the Lord your God is with you wherever you go."

It was His charge to me to go ahead with my plans. When God gives you what I will call "light" in this manner, do not neglect the moment. Don't ignore the light He gives you—that prompting or nudge in your spirit when you know He is speaking directly to you.

Make sure you understand Bible verses in the context of the entire Bible. In one sense, you want to *use the Bible to interpret the Bible.* Use the cross-reference system in the margins of the Bible to look up other similar verses. Use a concordance to more fully understand certain words. Read Christian books associated with the topic. Seek godly counsel. If you are making a major decision, you need to thoroughly understand everything God has to say about that subject. Do *not* pull one verse out of context and base your actions on that verse alone.

Circumstances

Favorable circumstances are usually an indicator that something may be a part of God's will for you, but don't rely completely on them. They need to line up with the Bible, godly counsel, and your heart's desire. Conversely, unfavorable circumstances do not always indicate that God is opposed to your plans. You may need to keep your heart's desire continually before the Lord even when no answer seems readily apparent. Keep seeking; keep praying. God will either change your heart, or He will change the circumstances. Beware of launching out on your own without some kind of signal or inner prompting from the Lord.

Godly Counsel

None of us by ourselves have all the wisdom, discernment, and knowledge needed to make the crucial decisions in life. The input of people who know us well—parents, godly friends, our pastor—is indispensable in deciding what God wants us to do with our future. My dad would be a good example of this. He was always particularly attuned to my needs and seemed to have the right word for me. I often went to him when I was feeling confused or perplexed about a situation, and he seemingly could speak to me in a way that cut right to the heart of the matter. I'm not necessarily talking about dramatic life events; he simply had this way of speaking that eased my burden and relieved tension in my life.

You will find that God has put certain people in your life you should always heed. They are indispensable to your spiritual well-being!

Repeated References

God, knowing that we can be slow to hear and even slower to understand, will sometimes emphasize an important point by doing us the courtesy of repeating it for us, usually in a relatively condensed period of time. For example, during your time alone with God, you might read a verse or passage that really hits home. Later that week you may call a friend to ask his opinion about a certain issue, and he mentions the same verse. Then you go to church on Sunday, and the pastor preaches about the very same verse! Wake up, believer! God is speaking to you, and you need to pay very close attention! Take notes if you have to, but don't forget His point!

Prophetic Words

After becoming Christians, some people are empowered by the Holy Spirit with supernatural gifts that enable them to hear directly from God about a certain person or situation. Among these gifts are the gift of prophecy, the word of wisdom, and the word of knowledge (see 1 Corinthians, chapters 12 through 14 for a more detailed description of all the spiritual gifts). There are some denominations of Christianity that believe these gifts were active only during the early, first-century church and do not exist today. With all due respect to their theologizing, I find nothing in God's Word to support that stance. In fact, I have been the personal beneficiary of a word of knowledge on two different occasions.

On one occasion, a person approached me in a church setting and said, "I have a word for you. You judge it," which was good advice because the Bible tells us to do exactly that—judge it—in that circumstance. It turned out to be a simple word of encouragement. On another occasion, I received a word regarding a very specific situation I was dealing with at the time. I had a career-related decision I had to make and was sensing I needed some input from the Lord, so this guidance arrived right on target. Even though the decision was not without risk, I was confident in the Lord's ability to land me in a good spot. I have also experienced one prophetic dream or "vision" that was fulfilled at a later point.

It is true that these gifts can be abused and misused, but

having seen them in action a few times, and believing that scripture testifies to their veracity, I can only conclude they are still active today. So, if you are ever in an environment where you encounter these gifts, it is wise to simultaneously be wary of your own skepticism but also be on the alert for someone who might be misusing these gifts. According to 1 Corinthians 14:29, it is our responsibility to "pass judgment" on any prophetic word spoken to us. Since the spirit of Christ is within us, He will aid us in discerning what *is*—and *is not*—from God.

State of Our Hearts

Listening to Our Hearts

Understanding our desires and motives is crucial to determining God's will for our lives. We need to have at least a rudimentary self-understanding of how we filter information and make decisions. I'm a "feeler," and thus a situation has to feel comfortable and inviting for me to proceed full steam ahead. All the details don't necessarily have to be lined up perfectly, but I need to be convinced that I am moving in a direction pleasing to God.

Speaking of details, we sometimes tie ourselves into a spiritual "knot" because we become overly neurotic about determining God's will for our lives. Keep it simple. Are you drawn to someone or some organization you might like to work with? Do you have some natural talent for the type of work you are interested in? These points of compatibility should be treated as open doors, and by all means, keep moving ahead toward your goals. If you happen to veer off course, God is perfectly capable of closing a door to a path that doesn't warrant further exploration.

Walking by Faith

What do we mean by that phrase? Above all else, we must understand that our faith in God's character, His goodness, that He is our shepherd and caretaker (see Psalm 23), is of paramount importance in life's journey. Maybe I believe more strongly than others about this subject, but when God opens a door, don't hesitate to walk through it. Keep moving forward (Philippians 3:13-14). As I previously stated, God will close a door if necessary, but I also believe He expects us to trust Him for the circumstances of our lives. As Proverbs 3:5-6 so aptly states, our role is to "trust" Him with all our hearts, to acknowledge His preeminence in every aspect of our lives, and it is His job to "make our paths straight." It is not our job to figure out the future, only to obey what we know.

The Mystery of God

One of the things we find difficult to accept is what I'm going to call the "mystery" of God. In our collective conceit, we think we should be able to have complete knowledge and understanding and to find a reasonable, rational explanation for all circumstances and outcomes in life. Not so. Our human perspective is very limited. We cannot see the big picture as God can, and we tend to define everything by how it feels to us at the moment.

To be honest, most of us will experience countless, sometimes unfortunate events in our lives for which no plausible explanation exists. We need endurance because, often, these experiences are accompanied by suffering, pain, or unrealized expectations, all of which can seem relentless in their quest to dislodge our trust in God. There are times when nothing seems comfortable or comforting, and we are tempted to turn to our own devices to fix the problem. Real trouble is potentially ahead, especially if our solution involves looking for ways to self-medicate or to escape dealing with the issue.

Suffering is an inescapable part of life, and I don't know anyone who is immune to it. Some of the pain we are in is self-inflicted because we are unaware of the impact sin can have on our psychological state. Every one of us is *a little bit twisted* as a result of sin. We can be oblivious to how deeply and profoundly it affects our interaction with others. Even our noblest actions are tainted with some degree of self-interest because we all struggle with the dichotomy of meeting the needs of others and, in turn, getting our own needs met.

In the midst of this dance, we often strain to protect our fragile sense of self and maintain some sense of control, however misguided that might be, but we often end up further distorting our perception of reality as we try to manipulate people and circumstances to get what we want. That obsession with control we are so prone to often comes at a cost to others and an even greater cost to ourselves if it causes us to turn *away from* God rather than *toward* Him.

We tend to approach God as if He owes us an explanation for life, the implication being He is indebted to us in some way, but that doesn't make sense since He is our benefactor. He gives His love to us free of charge, no strings attached. Hopefully, our response to His love will be to trust Him, as He has made us to function as creatures of faith: faith in His character and in His goodness. Do we understand that He has our best interests at heart in spite of everything and anything we might suffer (Romans 8:28)? The part of our nature that wants to cry out *"Why?"* when something adverse happens is in one sense a reflection of being God's creation. It's how we are wired, and because we have been created "in His image," we long to find reason, meaning, justice, and fairness in our world. It's only natural to ask questions like "Why do bad things happen to good people?" Most of us are very uncomfortable with that paradox, right? Not fair, right?

After being diagnosed with a fatal brain tumor, former Kansas City Royals pitcher Dan Quisenberry was asked if he ever thought, "Why me?" Quiz offered the most honest answer to that question I've ever heard: "Why *not* me?" he responded. Quiz understood that life is often a paradox, and even though paradoxes make us uncomfortable, they are nevertheless true and extant. God is three persons: Father, Son, and Holy Spirit—yet He is One, the great *I Am*. Do I understand that paradox? No, but I believe it, and I am willing to accept it because God is trustworthy and does not lie (Numbers 23:19).

Still, we need to respect the emotional turmoil of people who are struggling within the paradox of suffering; we need to stand with them as they work their way through the pain to move toward acceptance. After all, most of us seek out God because we want relief from the pain, not so we can experience more of it. Yes, it's easy to feel good about God when our lives are going well, but how do we respond when life takes an unexpected wrong turn and something bad happens, or, even worse, something *unfair* befalls us? While most of us have enough common sense to realize that suffering will occur at many points in our lives, and we are not immune to it or exempt from it, no one is standing in line asking for more. We don't welcome suffering; we try to avoid it.

Even though we know this to be true, we still struggle with accepting the emotional pain that comes with it because pain, as C.S. Lewis so aptly stated, is a problem.[20] Some people seem to receive more than their fair share of it, too, so who is responsible for that imbalance? To determine the heart of the issue, I think we need to sort out different types of suffering, some of which we can understand and some that come with no explanation.

In one sense, suffering because of the actions of another individual is the easiest to cope with because we can see who the "enemy" is, that is, we know who is responsible. Suffering can also be self-inflicted, which may take us a while to own up to depending on how honest we can be with ourselves. If we sin and suffer for it, then we have reaped only what we've sown, right? The degree of pain we experience also depends upon exactly *who* is affected by the suffering. I lost my younger brother Brian unexpectedly a few years ago, and it still hurts. That event continues to affect his family to this day. I still miss him. Why did that happen?

Two of my cousins were murdered in 1983. A deranged man entered their home very early one morning and went downstairs to their bedroom. He bludgeoned Janelle to death, abducted Kelly, raped and murdered her, and then dropped her body through a manhole into a snow-covered culvert where it was discovered several days later. Their brother Paul was severely beaten about the head; he survived but had to undergo extensive facial reconstruction.

I asked God why that happened, but I received no answer.

In our humanness, we feel the need to know "why," but more often than not, we are left with the pain of loss and silence from God. Even Jesus in His humanness asked God "why" as He died on the cross (Matthew 27:46), so we know it's not insanity on our part if we ask the question:

"My God, my God, why have You forsaken me?"

But even Jesus did not receive an answer, did He? When we are met with silence, it's so easy to become frustrated with God for His seeming indifference. I understand my cousins were the victim of one man's sinful actions, but that fact is of little comfort when we are trying to cope with the sorrow. In one sense, this event helps me to understand why God hates sin so deeply: It can *separate* us from each other, from our loved ones, and, ultimately, from God. Unfortunately, that separation is sometimes permanent and unfixable. Enduring this type of unexplained suffering is often the most severe of all tests of faith because there may be no resolution in this life. We must trust God to make it all right in the end.

The one person in the Bible who probably understood the struggle better than anyone else was Job. In chapter 1 of Job, we learn that he was "blameless, upright, fearing God, and turning away from evil." But tragedy strikes, and all of Job's children, servants, and livestock are killed in one horrible day. We would consider it a tragedy if we lost one child, but Job lost **all of them**! Then he became extremely ill. Can you imagine losing all of your family and then becoming ill to the point of death? It's no wonder Job's wife suggested he "curse God and die!" (Job 2:9).

Eventually, Job despaired of his life and wanted to die. He also began to question God's handling of his situation, even claiming that God had turned His back on him:

> I cry out to You for help, but You do not answer me;
> I stand up, and You turn Your attention against me.
> You have become cruel to me;
> With the might of Your hand You persecute me. (Job 30:20-21)

Did God understand Job's pain? Yes, but He also knew Job's limitations, humanness, and narrow understanding of the bigger picture:

> "Now gird up your loins like a man; I will ask you, and you instruct Me. Will you really annul My judgment? Will you condemn Me that you may be justified? Pour out the overflowings of your anger; And look on everyone who is proud, and make him low. Look on everyone who is proud, and humble him and tread down the wicked where they stand…Then I will also confess to you, that your own right hand can save you." (Job 40:7-8; 11-12; 14)

In essence, God is basically asking Job if he thinks he is qualified to do His job, to be the ultimate Judge, to decide who falls and who stands justified. Does Job understand how the universe works and is he qualified to dispense perfect justice? Job responds and admits to God that he doesn't want His job after all, and that he lacks the understanding and wisdom needed to discharge the duties of the office even if he did want it. God eventually restores all of Job's losses, and he ends up with an even larger family than he possessed before the calamity.

This restoration of Job's good fortune is a picture of eternity for all believers who will read his story. We may suffer loss, persecution, and unbearable heartbreak during our lives on earth, but, for those believers who love God and are willing to put their lives in His hands, there awaits a "restoration" job in heaven, a permanent healing for all the temporary loss we will suffer in our lifetime.

14
DO WE HAVE THE RIGHT TO JUDGE OTHERS?

IN THE SPRING of 2016, 49 people were killed in a mass shooting at a gay nightclub in Orlando, Florida. The shooter claimed allegiance to the terrorist group ISIS. This event precipitated responses from numerous sources, many of whom seemed to fancy themselves as self-appointed judges of the gay lifestyle. We heard different voices attributing this act to God. Some people said this was the wrath of God upon the LGBT community, His judgment upon their lifestyle, as if He personally sent that mad man in there to extinguish lives.

It's amazing to find people so ready to explain God's intentions toward gay people. Isn't it presumptuous, even arrogant, to claim that we know the mind of God regarding this matter? In fact, I believe Jesus issued a very pointed warning in the Bible about the consequences of judging others.

> "Do not judge, so that you will not be judged. For in the way you judge, you will be judged; and by your standard of measure, it will be measured to you. Why do you look at the speck that is in your brother's eye, but do not notice the log that is in your own eye?" (Matthew 7:1-3)

When I look at my life, I see cause for concern when I read this verse. Frankly, all you would have to do to find out how deeply flawed and sinful I am is to display my every thought on an electronic billboard for the whole world to see. I doubt it would take you more than 30 minutes to conclude that I'm not the person I need to be. Now if God administered punishment to me according to my sins (especially my sinful thoughts), I've got news for you: He would have vaporized me a long time ago. Given that my condition is common to, oh, about 100 percent of the population (all perfect people, please disregard the preceding statement), when anyone, especially a believer in God, steps forward and condemns others by telling them they are the recipients of God's wrath, they are embarrassing all who call upon the name of God. *Who appointed them as judge?*

Do we not understand that God punished humankind's sin two thousand years ago on the cross? Jesus bore the punishment for all sin, *once for all people* (1 Peter 3:18)—past, present, and future. Until God closes the book when Christ returns at the end of the age, the forgiveness He purchased by His death is available to *all* living persons, including people struggling with their sexual identity. His judgment has been suspended until His return occurs, and we dare not sit in the seat of judgment, for in doing so, we dishonor God and the sacrificial death of Jesus Christ. Yes, it is true that if people ultimately reject the truth of Christ's death for their sins, *they will be judged* for their failure to acknowledge Jesus as Savior:

> ...when the Lord Jesus shall be revealed from heaven with His mighty angels in flaming fire, dealing out retribution **to those who do not know God** and to those who do not obey the gospel of our Lord Jesus. These will pay the penalty of eternal destruction, away from the presence of the Lord and from the glory of His power. (2 Thessalonians 1:7b-9)

As this scripture says, the only people who will ultimately pay the price for their sin are those who "do not know God...those who do not obey the gospel of our Lord Jesus." Christ died for our sins; that is the truth that saves us from judgment. This offer of eternal life is open to all people who believe in Christ, no matter what their current state may be. If you choose to reject God's gift, then yes, you will stand alone before Him with no one to plead your case. Bear in mind that God's standard for acceptance into heaven is unblemished holiness—absolute perfection. That is what is required to enter heaven if you wish to stand before Him on the basis of your own goodness. I pray you will not make that choice. Remember the electronic billboard that I mentioned?

Regarding the Orlando event, contrary to what the self-appointed arbiters of judgment said, God is not running around dispensing wrath in the form of terrorist attacks and mass executions, and if we tell people God is punishing them for their sin, we completely occlude the Gospel of Christ. When we take up the mantle of judgment, we are seen as haters. Consequently, we invite the world to hate God because we claim to speak for Him. We become as the Pharisees (the religious people of Jesus's day), who so grieved Him with their self-righteous judgment of others.

In addition to not sitting in the seat of judgment, believers need be smart and understand the prism through which people view them. The LGBT community may often view believers as bigoted accusers and judges. If we try to approach them by making blanket statements about God's wrath, they understandably go into defensive mode. We then become ministers of condemnation instead of ministers of reconciliation, regardless of what our intent was. So, don't approach others as their judge; approach them as a fellow human being who has your own particular set of sinful tendencies to deal with (the billboard again), and then point them to Christ for help and healing. Step out of the role of judge, and let the one true Judge handle it. How can we who have met Christ, who have tasted of His mercy, not extend it to others?

Were the people in that bar sinners? Yes, they were and are, as we all are. Is it our responsibility to heap condemnation upon them? Most emphatically, "No!" The last time I checked God's Word, our role is to let others know what Christ has done for them, to let them know that He has paid the ransom for their souls. But we commit a grave error when we posture up as holy people and pretend that we speak for God in the midst of these tragedies. We desperately need to shift our perspective. Proverbs 11:2 says:

> When pride comes, then comes dishonor, but with the humble is wisdom.

The Hebrew word translated as "pride" in this passage is "*zadown*."[21] It refers to the kind of pride that presumes to have more authority than is warranted. Believers are called to be more tactful, more gracious in their approach.

> Therefore, we are ambassadors for Christ, as though God were making an appeal through us; we beg you on behalf of Christ, be reconciled to God. (2 Corinthians 5:20)

Believers must not exercise judgment over others but instead point them to God, who alone is qualified to pass judgment on their behavior. People will bait you with invitations to step into the role of judge, but you must resist the temptation to do so. On more than one occasion I have had someone put it to me like this: "So, if I did _____ to this person, am I going to hell?" Fill in the blank with any misdeed you wish; it's still a trap for those who want to be reconcilers.

Be aware that people sometimes pose these types of questions because they are setting up a straw man they can then knock down with one blow. If you answer their question about hell with a "yes," then they quickly slip into the role of the victimized innocent, claiming that "no god who loves us would send someone to hell." This allows them to completely dismiss the idea of a just, true God by labeling Him as cruel, harsh judge for sending them to hell. In this fashion, they avoid any serious discussion about God by denigrating His character, and they avoid taking responsibility for the state of their relationship with Him. The straw man falls once again.

This is a favorite tactic of one such political jester who has a network show but shall remain nameless here. He knocks down that same straw man time and time again by first reminding you that he has read the Bible, which, on the surface, is commendable. I have heard him state in so many words that he cannot accept a god who has committed genocide (presumably, he is referring to the instances where God wipes out His people Israel's enemies in the Old Testament). Lamentably, he is only citing the portion of the Bible he can use to justify his argument, while conveniently ignoring the part where God establishes a new covenant and provides forgiveness to *all of humankind* through the death of His Son on the cross. Oh, the power of selective reasoning! Like any good debater, he is only trying to win the argument.

The antidote to our "judgment" dilemma is to avoid overstepping our place in the affairs of God.

We must never sit in the seat of judgment when a nonbeliever is involved.

I once spoke with a man who had an effective ministry to the gay community. His answer to the question about hell or any other question regarding judgment was to step out of the way and point that person to God. When some people would ask him if he believed they were going to hell because of their homosexuality, he would say something to this effect: "I personally have no problem with your lifestyle or the choices you make." This statement effectively disarmed his listener, in the sense that the person he was talking to did not feel they were being judged by him. After pausing to let them digest his first statement, he would follow up by saying something similar to this: "However, God feels this way about your lifestyle, and it is Him to whom you are accountable, to whom you must answer."

By simultaneously stepping out of the role of judge and acknowledging that this role belongs only to God, he was loving the people he talked to by pointing them directly to God. This attitude opened the door for further discussions regarding their faith and their future.

The tendency of believers to judge people who don't pledge any fidelity to any god is alarming to say the least. Several issues lie at the root of this attitude, but I believe the most common one is plain, old religious pride: thinking we are better than someone else simply because we identify with or supposedly "belong" to some religious establishment. Could be a church, a mosque, or a cult—the outward trappings do not matter if we are using them to masquerade as another person's judge. We must wake up and realize that God is not impressed by the show. He is looking for substance:

> ...for God sees not as man sees, for man looks at the outward appearance, but the Lord looks at the heart. (1 Samuel 16:7b)

Believers are delusional if they think they will get away with this stale brand of hypocrisy. God is not fooled, and neither are "real" people. The Pharisees, who were supposedly the religious rulers and teachers of the Jews in Jesus's day, were constantly flaunting their religiosity in front of others:

> "When you pray, you are not to be like the hypocrites; for they love to stand and pray in the synagogues and on the street corners so that they may be seen by men. Truly I say to you, they have their reward in full." (Matthew 6:5)

Jesus is saying we should be careful of basing our worth on how highly we can make others think of us because we are *not* being measured on the praise accorded us by men. God is judging us based on the motives of our hearts. If the glory of men is more important to us than God's approval, then that is *all* we will receive, both in this life and the next. Whatever we are putting our trust in to win the approval of men—be it fame, riches, social status, or religion—please understand: These things are worthless in God's eyes. If He were keeping a scorecard on our performance, it would have nothing but zeroes on it. Mine would too.

What then does God want from us? He wants action that is motivated by the love of God, by allegiance to Him. If our motives are not based on pleasing God, then all that work and striving to please man will result in dissipation. It will not pass the litmus test of proper motive; it will not go with us into eternity.

> According to the grace of God which was given to me, like a wise master builder I laid a foundation, and another is building on it. But each man must be careful how he builds on it. For no man can lay a foundation other than the one which is laid, which is Jesus Christ. Now if any man builds on the foundation with gold, silver, precious stones, wood, hay, straw, each man's work will become evident; for the day will show it because it is to be revealed with fire, and the fire itself will test the quality of each man's work. If any man's work which he has built on it remains, he will receive a reward. If any man's work is burned up, he will suffer loss; but he himself will be saved, yet so as through fire. (1 Corinthians 3:10-15)

As the Apostle Paul indicates in verse 14, our ill-motivated actions, such as judging others, will not survive, especially if we are doing it to make us feel superior or better than others. We will not have anything to offer to God when we enter into His presence. That sobering fact should cause us to examine our lives for evidence that proves we have loved God and our fellow man. Please consider Paul's heartfelt instructions to the Corinthians:

> If I speak with the tongues of men and of angels, but do not have love, I have become a noisy gong or a clanging cymbal. If I have the gift of prophecy, and know all mysteries and all knowledge; and if I have all faith, so as to remove mountains, but do not have love, I am nothing. And if I give all my possessions to feed the poor, and if I surrender my body to be burned, but do not have love, it profits me nothing. (1 Corinthians 13:1-3)

Based on this passage, there is a simple test we can administer to see if what we are doing in this life will pass muster with God: Is it motivated by love? It sounds simple, but even our most noble actions can arise from a corrupt heart. Even something as innocent as leading a Bible study or service project can turn into an exercise in self-glorification if we are not diligent in examining the motives of our hearts. If most of us were honest about what lies beneath the surface, we would have to admit to a tendency to give in order to get. We want to serve others, but we would also like to be highly thought of by our peers and friends.

At times, a bit of ego is thrown into the mix, which can even contaminate our inner life with the Lord if we are not watchful.

15
Is the Bible True?

Is the Bible, which claims to be the true Word of God, the only communication we have from God? What about the other spiritual books out there? I believe the Bible is the singular, true Word of God, and I submit to you that life itself is the best evidence for not only the exclusivity but also the veracity of the Bible. I have yet to see a single word of the Bible disproved, and as I continue reading it nearly every day, I am discovering new scriptural truths that heretofore have escaped my notice. Other books or writings may contain elements of truth, but that doesn't mean God was their author.

The Bible is unique among all books in that it is imbued with the supernatural power of God. When I read it, I am touched in the deepest part of my being and spirit, in such a way that I am motivated to set about changing, or at least examining, my thoughts, behavior, and future plans. The Bible is profoundly simple on some levels, so simple that a child can understand its message, but it also holds up under intense scrutiny. You can go as deep as you want to go in exploring its riches, and you will never exhaust the truth and wisdom it contains.

The most powerful evidence for the Bible is life itself because our real-life experiences testify to what is both prescribed and described in its pages. I can willfully put into practice what is prescribed there, and it really works, or I can live life, and then go back to the Bible, and find my daily experience in the world reflected back to me in the truth it contains. It seems odd to say this, but the Bible is almost "scientific" in that you can figuratively apply to it the scientific method. This is an imperfect illustration, but please extend me some latitude to make a point:

1. **Postulate**—The Bible is the true Word of God.
2. **Proof**—I can live life according to the precepts found in God's Word (and it works!), and I can also find my daily experience reflected back to me as I read it.
3. **Theorem**—The Bible must be the Word of God because all real-life evidence supports the principles it espouses.

For the purpose of illustration, let me say that I see similarities between, say, the Bible and, for example, the principle of gravity. You drop an apple from an apple tree one thousand times, and, one thousand times, it falls to the ground and rests in contact with the earth's surface. You read the Bible, live life every day, and everything you experience is reflected somewhere in the pages of God's Word. Does that mean your every *question* receives a specific answer? No, but if you go to Him, God will give you the peace you need to sustain yourself through the trials of life. Frankly, there are some questions we will not receive answers to on this side of heaven, but take heart, resolution will come one day.

Before all the scientists and naturalists reading this run screaming from the room, I want to share some of my favorite verses from the Bible and describe how they relate to our lives:

<u>Psalm 42:1-2</u>

**As the deer pants for the water brooks,
So my soul pants for You, O God.
My soul thirsts for God, for the living God;
When shall I come and appear before God?**

I always come back to this one and have memorized it for that reason. More than any other verse in the Bible, it defines how I feel about life on this earth, difficult as it may be sometimes. From my perspective, I am constantly thirsting to be in the presence of God but never quite able to get all the way there. Though I may seek to be close to God through prayer and worship, it often feels like I catch only fleeting glimpses of Him. At times, it seems that life itself, with its responsibilities, burdens, and distractions, is an impediment blocking our path to God.

This mysterious longing to make contact with God always remains, even on my best days worshiping Him or talking to Him. To some extent, I will always feel like the deer, peering intently through the foliage, trying to find that elusive river of water where my thirst will be satisfied by God's presence. This longing and vague sense of always being in need, of always looking for something greater than myself to define my life, will always be with me as long as I am imprisoned in this mortal body. I long to be with Jesus, and the longing is always there, and I can never be fully satisfied until I am with Him. Then and only then will I be completely free of my limitations—self-imposed or otherwise—and finally thirst no longer.

Psalm 130:5

I wait for the Lord, my soul does wait,
And in His word do I hope.

My experience with God has taught me to be patient, to wait on God, especially when someone seems to be demanding a decision out of me. People love to choose sides, but as believers, we have to resist the temptation to be a people pleaser who passively acquiesces to whatever someone is demanding of them. Conversely, you cannot shrink from confronting the issue or request at hand. When we feel undue pressure to come down on one side or the other, we have to hold firm to Christ. People will demand that we come over to their side in the name of loyalty, but we must be loyal to

Christ first of all, and then people's needs will fall in line behind Him; they will be managed by Him. Nothing must disturb the believer's loyalty to the One who owns him or her.

> No soldier in active service entangles himself in the affairs of everyday life, so that he may please the one who enlisted him as a soldier. (2 Timothy 2:4)

1 Timothy 1:5

But the goal of our instruction is love from a pure heart and a good conscience and a sincere faith.

I love this verse because even though we may learn so much as a Christian, the goal is not to accumulate knowledge but to learn to love people, as opposed to judging them. God always grounds us when we start to think too highly of ourselves or too lowly of others. We are disgusted at this or that person and their ugly behavior, unable to give them any grace or mercy, but if we look closely enough at our hearts, we find out how substandard and reprehensible our thoughts and actions can be. Pride is truly an abomination to God, and if we insist on having our own way with everyone and everything, then He will let us make an unholy mess of our lives. In truth, He wants to eradicate pride from our souls. He wants to extinguish it.

That may sound extreme, but look at the many confrontations between Jesus and the Pharisees (the Jewish religious leaders of the day) in the gospels. On multiple occasions, He verbally undresses them for their by-the-letter-of-the-law, holier-than-thou arrogance, skewering their pompous, smug religiosity as He goes. The truth is, though, you don't have to be a Pharisee to be plagued by this sin. It's pretty much a universal condition. I can't remember how many times in my thoughts I have maligned people (most of the time I haven't got the courage to say it to their face) and then discovered the same defect in myself only hours or days later. The Lord will bring us up against pride every time until we realign our thinking and become slow, very slow, to anger—and even slower to judge. He is teaching us to love rather than to pass judgment on others. He can supply all the correction they need. We are here to love both friends and enemies, and that is all.

Proverbs 18:21

**Death and life are in the power of the tongue,
And those who love it will eat its fruit.**

James 3:8-9

But no one can tame the tongue; it is a restless evil and full of deadly poison. With it we bless our Lord and Father, and with it we curse men, who have been made in the likeness of God.

"Sticks and stones may break my bones, but words will never hurt me."

That was what we said as kids, but we were so wrong. We knew it then, and we know it now. We spend a great portion of our lives wielding words like a scimitar, cutting people up with them, tossing word grenades over the wall, sending that perfect little dig, so people would know exactly how we feel. Then we gasp in surprise when that grenade gets tossed back over the wall by a person we have wounded with a perfectly placed snipe. Next—an explosion, leaving both parties a bloody mess.

The truth is that our emotions get the best of us more times than not, and we are left to clean up the debris, verbal scars, wounded feelings, and mess. Maybe if we could see the impact our words will have before they escape our lips, that would help. Proverbs 18:21 is a great help because it reminds me of how powerful my words are. They are either death, or they are life. I can speak death to a person, or I can speak life to them. We are to be careful with our words because they have an *effect* on people. There is nothing wrong with letting people know how we feel, but we must remember that our words reveal what is in our hearts. If our hearts are bad, or mad, the fruit produced by our words will most likely be rotten as well.

Proverbs 25:11

Like apples of gold in settings of silver
Is a word spoken in right circumstances.

Proverbs 16:23-24

The heart of the wise instructs his mouth
And adds persuasiveness to his lips.
Pleasant words are a honeycomb,
Sweet to the soul and healing to the bones.

Proverbs 15:1-2

A gentle answer turns away wrath,
But a harsh word stirs up anger.
The tongue of the wise makes knowledge acceptable,
But the mouth of fools spouts folly.

In contrast to the verses that explain how destructive our tongue *can* be, the opposite result can be achieved when we use words that edify and build others up. It pays to think before you speak, right? The business world is an excellent teacher in this regard because in that milieu we experience plenty of stress and potential conflict, especially if we don't guard what we both speak and write. Anyone receive any angry emails lately?

I can recall one instance when I was sitting in a meeting with management and several supervisors discussing completion dates for production jobs. Our final assembly supervisor took his turn speaking and proceeded to describe how production scheduling (that would be me) had overscheduled his area, thus making it impossible to complete the given schedule on time. He didn't stop there. He made his way through a whole list of other problems I had created for his department. He was definitely getting under my skin, and I was busy thinking through my defense as he recited the litany of offenses I had committed. As I was about to begin speaking in my own defense, the Holy Spirit stopped me short before I could even open my mouth. He apprehended me, held me up, you might say. Instead of defending myself, I took a deep breath, looked him in the eye, and said, "What can I do to improve the way I'm doing things?"

He was stunned into silence for a moment, and then he made some suggestions. The meeting proceeded full steam ahead, and I took his advice to heart. I think the way I responded to him disarmed his anger, and the whole discussion turned out to be very productive. I would like to think the aforementioned verses from Proverbs influenced my reaction that day.

Jeremiah 29:11-13

"For I know the plans that I have for you," declares the Lord, "plans for welfare and not for calamity, to give you a future and a hope. Then you will call upon Me and come and pray to Me, and I will listen to you. You will seek Me and find Me when you search for Me with all your heart."

Christians often cite this verse as proof of God's good intentions toward us (and that it is), but I think we often forget that it's a two-sided coin in that God expects us to seek Him out as well as enjoy Him. He is looking for a little dialogue here, right? I know I tend to be very content to bask in the glow of knowing God, often worrying about whether or not God is blessing me as I want Him to, rather than earnestly seeking Him first before I create my laundry list of requests. We are very quick to complain when life becomes challenging, but we are not so quick to seek God in the midst of our everyday life. I sometimes wonder how much we would seek Him if life really was a cakewalk, if all our problems were removed before we got out of bed. I mean, I'm not very good at the seeking part now, so why would I even bother if everything was easy and smooth?

We ask why God allows pain and suffering, but could it be that the circumstances I hate and try so desperately to avoid might actually be serving me well as the only reason I seek God in the first place? They drive me to Him, which is good, right? What pain tells us is that faith is only a word until the test comes: Will I still trust God's intentions despite how bad this experience feels? Will I allow it to drive me away *from* God—or *toward* Him?

No one is exempt from suffering when you get right down to it. For the most part, I've had a nice, comfortable life, but it's had its share of heartache and disappointment too. Consider this: We who live in the United States barely have to worry about our physical needs, which is a major life issue for one third of the world's population. That brings us to another issue: We have it so good that our financial comfort and security can be a hindrance to our relationship with the Lord. We are not in any need, so we don't feel compelled to seek Him.

Maybe if I missed a few meals I might be a little hungrier for God. Maybe if I emptied my hands and let go of some "stuff," I might feel closer to Him.

Whatever our circumstances—good or difficult—we have to find a way to stay in touch with our Creator because that relationship is the very stuff of life.

16
DISTINGUISHING BETWEEN PUNISHMENT AND DISCIPLINE

ALL OF US have some grasp of the fine line that exists between punishment and discipline, since we all had a childhood, regardless of whether or not we became parents. No doubt everyone has an opinion as to how well our parents or caretakers divided the two categories. Maybe we thought they were harsh or unfair at times, but hopefully some of our eyes have been opened far enough to appreciate how difficult a job they had in parenting us.

Of course, as kids, we played our own part in the family dramas that resulted from collisions with them over what was "fair" and what was "right." Typically, every kid learns what they can and can't get away with by pushing their parents to—or past—the limits of whatever guidelines they prescribed, all of which were presumably for our benefit.

We learned we could manipulate our parents and play them against each other, and, unfortunately, we also learned to prey on their weakness of will or conviction in certain choice areas. Do we try to use these same techniques on God? If so, we are sorely deluded, for God Almighty cannot be manipulated with any degree of success whatsoever. Given that, why doesn't He come down hard on us every time we misbehave or mistreat someone?

God fully understands the set of problems our earthly parents experienced. His children are naturally rebellious, stubborn, self-centered, unforgiving, deceitful, and very likely to choose the path of least resistance in getting what they want from life and people. Some of us approach God in the same fashion as we did our parents, trying to game Him by stretching or ignoring the boundaries of the Bible. Or even worse, many of us are unjustifiably ignorant and don't even know what limits or moral imperatives God is asking us to live by in the first place. We are playing at "religion," picking and choosing what is convenient to live by and carelessly omitting anything else. We can unwittingly become hypocrites by playing this game.

Yet, here is the strange thing. In contrast to our parents, when God disciplines us, most of the time we are not aware that it is coming directly from His own hand. We might blame other people for it, or, if we are honest, we might recognize that what we suffer as a result of our disobedience to God's truth consists primarily of the natural consequences of whatever sin we are prone to indulge in. We reap what we sow, correct? Hopefully, all of us have discovered the negative results of sin.

What escapes our notice is how often we get away with it with no obvious consequences. Could it be that God is far more merciful than we realize because we get away with—or at least we think we are getting away with—far more than we should. Of course, taking responsibility for one's own actions seemingly has become a sign of weakness in our modern culture. It appears far better to assume the mantle of "victim" and complain incessantly about how mistreated, abused, or unfortunate we are. We act the same way with God.

Thankfully, our Father in heaven will have none of that ruse. He holds us accountable for all behavior, both good and bad, even if we manage to escape the real-world consequences of our sin. As our perfect, loving Father, He must be an inerrant judge of our actions and yet still be able to love us unconditionally. He has to practice *perfect tough love*.

Therein lies the balancing act, for how does God provide the discipline we need without mixing it with anger and punishment? We receive insight as to how He works in this passage from Hebrews 12:7-11:

> It is for discipline that you endure; God deals with you as with sons; for what son is there whom his father does not discipline? But if you are without discipline, of which all have become partakers, then you are illegitimate children and not sons. Furthermore, we had earthly fathers to discipline us, and we respected them; shall we not much rather be subject to the Father of spirits, and live? For they disciplined us for a short time as seemed best to them, but He disciplines us for our good, so that we may share His holiness. All discipline for the moment seems not to be joyful, but sorrowful; yet to those who have been trained by it, afterwards it yields the peaceful fruit of righteousness.

In verse 8, we learn that God's discipline is real, tangible evidence that we belong to Him, that we are His beloved child. His discipline is not without purpose, either, for He is using it to change us from the inside out, to conform our character to that of Christ, "so that we may share His holiness" (verse 10).

Fortunately for us, even though we, as believers, as children of God, are still prone to struggle with the same sins time after time—some maybe for an entire lifetime—God does not abandon disciplining us in favor of outright punishment. In Psalm 30:5, we are given a glimpse of how God deals with His oft-wayward children:

> For His anger is but for a moment,
> His favor is for a lifetime;
> Weeping may last for the night,
> But a shout of joy comes in the morning.

Mercy triumphs over judgment. This is the defining trait of our heavenly Father, God, the one who pardons our iniquities, who forgives our every sin. Frankly, to experience the mercy of God on an ongoing, day-by day basis is one of the most awe-inspiring facets of His character. My personal experience has convinced me of God's incredibly patient, tolerant, and merciful nature. No wonder, then, that He asks us to show the same consideration to others:

> He has told you, O man, what is good;
> And what does the Lord require of you
> But to do justice, to love kindness,
> And to walk humbly with your God. (Micah 6:8)

Since God punished all of humankind's sin on the cross, we are now free to experience the mercy of God, which opens the door for relationship with Him as we enjoy the fullness of a life lived with and for someone who cares deeply about us.

But doesn't God have limits? There must be a point past which we dare not push Him. We first need to examine our own lives before we look too closely at those around us, but if we see a fellow believer engaged in sin, we need to confront them. We should proceed with caution and be sure we have made our concerns known to at least one other person who cares about the individual in question. The reason for this is to make sure we are reading the situation accurately, so bouncing it off another trustworthy believer helps us to confirm what we think we are seeing. After all, we cannot judge another person's heart; we can only look at the outward actions as a way of interpreting what's going on inside. Hence, the opinion of at least one other believer will aid us in confirming we are in line with God's view of the person's heart, which, fortunately, is perfectly clear and not subject to any human distortion:

> ...for God sees not as man sees, for man looks at the outward appearance, but the Lord looks at the heart. (1 Samuel 16:7b)

So, where exactly is the point of no return, that point of disobedience where God finally says, "That's enough"?

God's patience with us seems boundless and limitless, but can we exhaust that patience if we don't heed the warning signs He is so sure to provide for us? The responsibility lies with us. We need to make sure we never get to the point where God is forced to resort to extreme measures, as in the Apostle Paul's recounting of two unfortunate fellows he had to deal with in a severe manner:

> This command I entrust to you, Timothy, my son, in accordance with the prophecies previously made concerning you, that by them you fight the good fight, keeping faith and a good conscience, which some have rejected and suffered shipwreck in regard to their faith. **Among these are Hymenaeus and Alexander, whom I have handed over to Satan, so that they will be taught not to blaspheme.** (1 Timothy 1:18-20)

Paul's comments may seem severe, but he was dealing with two men who had exhausted God's patience and had put themselves in a situation requiring certain consequences. These men had suffered "shipwreck" in regards to their faith, and something extraordinary was required as a result.

May we never find ourselves in their position.

17

THE ART OF THANKFUL SERVICE

OVER THE YEARS, I have offered more than a few desperate prayers to the Lord. He has answered some of them in the affirmative, some not. Many of them continue to be ongoing concerns for which the answer lies more in the journey than in a final solution. However our prayers are answered, we need be mindful of our reaction—or lack thereof—to what God does or doesn't do in our lives.

Recently, I attended an afternoon baseball game to cheer on my home team, the Kansas City Royals. After arriving at the game, my first thought was to get a bottle of water, as the temperature was in the mid-90s already and expected to become hotter. I arrived at the front of the line, pulled out my wallet, and was shocked to see my driver's license, credit card, and a whole slew of other cards missing from their customary front-slot position.

I'm sure you know what that moment of abject terror feels like when you discover something *that* important is not where it should be. I went ahead and watched some of the game, but I left early to start retracing my steps that day. Maybe they slipped out when I went through the security checkpoint at the stadium, or maybe I left them at Target where I had stopped before the game to pick up sunscreen? I even called my boss back at work to have him check my desk to see if I had left them there. I was sick about it because my backtracking turned up nothing, and I was feeling pretty desperate.

"Lord, please, if I lost them, please let them fall into the hands of a righteous person who will return them."

That was my first prayer, followed by more mini-prayers.

I finally went on home and told my wife Shirley what had happened, and she was so sweet about it. "That could have happened to any one of us, Honey," she said. She urged me to retrace my steps for the past few days, so I committed to that exercise, and wouldn't you know it, I remembered a trip to Wal-Mart only a few days earlier that was kind of harried, and I kind of vaguely remembered fiddling with my wallet there. I made the call, and they had my cards!! At first it was intense relief I felt, but then I dropped to my knees and thanked the Lord for the way this fiasco turned out. I kept thanking Him as the evening wore on and even the next morning during my prayer time. The catch is this: Will I remember this event a year from now? Will it be supplanted by some other significant event? Will I remember how the Lord took care of this for me? The key is remembering. God constantly adjured the Israelites to "remember."

> You shall remember all the way which the Lord your God has led you in the wilderness these forty years, that He might humble you, testing you, to know what was in your heart, whether you would keep His commandments or not. (Deuteronomy 8:2)

The Israelites were not very good at recalling the Lord God's track record. In fact, they needed constant reminders and several path-corrective measures to keep their attention. Hopefully, we can learn from their example and stop to take time to thank God when life is going well—as well as when it isn't. Now, that's the challenge: to be thankful even when our circumstances are less than ideal, or when we encounter adversarial people, or when we simply don't feel like being thankful.

How easy it is to fall into the habit of grumbling about everything while appreciating nothing. Driving seems to bring out the worst in me, and I'm sure I'm not alone in that respect. Something happens when I sit behind the wheel, and seldom is it pretty to watch. I tend to behave as if I were the master of the universe and my fellow drivers were all obstacles in my path to my chosen destination. I'm waiting for someone to do something I don't like. I really have to stop and mentally overhaul my attitude from time to time because it's not worth it, and it's not pleasing to the Lord. Good grief, just relax and go with the flow. So what if somebody cuts you off on the highway? Why expend the anger and ruin your day or someone else's day? Thank God for whatever delays or obstacles you encounter in traffic. Who knows, maybe they helped you avoid an accident along the way.

No matter what challenges we encounter during our daily grind, we need to exercise humility and kindness. "In everything give thanks; for this is God's will for you in Christ Jesus," is what Paul told the Thessalonians, and we need to put that thought into constant practice (1 Thessalonians 5:18).

One practical expression of thanksgiving lies in our attitude toward serving God and others. Are we here looking to be waited on, or are we looking to wait on others? Now, it is true that Jesus served His disciples by way of demonstration. He assumed the role of servant, washing His disciples' feet. Does that mean we should all line up for our foot-washing? Not exactly. Jesus did this to demonstrate to His disciples how they ought to treat their fellow man. If God washes our feet, then we certainly should wash the feet of others.

The Lord has provided me with some unforgettable examples of what that should look like. One such demonstration occurred while on the way to a Presbyterian camp in Parkville, Missouri, to attend a men's retreat sponsored by my church. On the bus, I happened to sit next to an extremely friendly guy whom I didn't know, but we struck up a conversation about God anyway. Come to find out that he was going to be the speaker for the weekend! Really nice guy, I thought, as we got off the bus to unload our luggage. We were dragging the bags out from beneath the bus when he quickly grabbed mine, turned to me, and said, "Here, let me get that for you." Before I could even respond, he grabbed my bag and carried it into the cabin, while I stood there empty-handed and slightly dumbfounded.

I stood there a little longer, until the light finally came on. Here was the speaker for the retreat—someone you would normally think of as being above bellboy status—picking up my bag for me without ever being asked to do it. "Okay, Lord," I thought, *"I think I get it."* Time slowed down as God took a small, isolated moment and amplified it with meaning, making me aware of what it truly meant to be a servant of others. This little exchange probably didn't take more than thirty seconds, but I will never forget it. It impacted me to a degree totally disproportionate to the situation. I probably learned more in that one moment than I could have from reading five books on the subject.

We are fortunate to serve a God who will *teach* us the principles of servanthood and thankfulness even if we fail to cultivate those qualities ourselves. I can't boast of a robust prayer life, but I want to share what I've learned regarding how to approach the Lord with an attitude grounded in thankfulness and earnest petition. Periodically, you have to seek God's ear; you have to really *plead* with Him. He places great value on the ***sincerity*** of your prayers. You might even say He is looking for some ***passion***, some real emotional investment in what you are asking. He wants to know how much you care, and oh, by the way, He is much more interested in *people*, as opposed to situations you want to see changed. Hebrews 11:6 puts it this way:

> And without faith it is impossible to please Him, for he who comes to God must believe that He is and that He is a rewarder of those who seek Him.

So, part of faith is having confidence in the Lord's promise to reward us when we put our hearts into it. I once had the opportunity to lead the discussion in a Sunday School class when the regular leader was gone. Instead of praying about leading well, I decided to start praying for the individuals in the class. I prayed intensely for those people—that God would bless them and give them something that would make a difference in their lives—and I meant it. I thanked God for each one of them. I really wanted them to receive something for the time they invested studying God's Word. My point is that the prayer wasn't about me or even having a good class discussion. It was about the individuals I was serving. *They* are what matters to the Lord, not my success or adequacy as a discussion leader.

Something very interesting occurred when the class commenced later that morning. I opened up with a brief introduction of the biblical text and then asked only one question. The discussion that ensued was notably vivid with people sharing stories about their lives and citing people and passages from the Bible that had influenced their thinking. It was awesome to witness because, other than one brief comment, all I did was listen! Comments were flying so fast and furious that I really didn't need to say anything at all. God took over, opening people's hearts up, loosening their inhibitions, and I simply sat there for 35 minutes listening. Finally, I said, "Thank you all for coming. We need to wrap things up here because the service is about ready to start." It was an amazing experience watching God open people's hearts.

Now, whenever I pray, I exercise my faith in God by putting some energy, sincerity, and heart into it. I strive to mean it, being passionate before the Lord about His people and pleading with the Lord to make a difference in people's lives. I think He respects that prayer—the prayer focused on the needs of those we are serving. Owing to this experience, I now make a point of prioritizing prayer over preparation when I am teaching and/or facilitating discussions of God's Word, no matter the circumstances. I truly believe that five to 10 minutes of heartfelt prayer for those we are leading is as important as an hour of preparation. Make a habit of it.

When we see God work like this, the results should be followed by a deep sense of gratitude on our part. Give Him some feedback. We don't want to be like the lepers who Jesus healed in Luke 17:12-19, only one of whom turned back to thank Jesus after He had healed all 10 of them. When the Lord answers prayer, we should answer back by giving Him thanks and appreciating our benefactor.

We should view serving others as an expression of gratitude for the love God has already expended on us.

18
POSITIVE SUFFERING

The gift of eternal life is absolutely free, but it will cost you your life.
-Anonymous

AFTER THE APOSTLE Paul was smitten blind on the road to Damascus (see the book of Acts in the New Testament), he was directed to enter the city and wait for further instruction. God then told a man named Ananias to go and tell Paul that God was going to "show him (Paul) how much he must suffer for My name's sake" (Acts 9:16). Now, that is not a normal statement to make to a new hire when he or she first comes on board. So, Jesus suffered, and His chief ambassador Paul was going to suffer.

Where does that leave you and me and the rest of His disciples in the pecking order? To top it off, Jesus made statements like: *"He who loves his life loses it,"* and *"He who hates his life in this world shall keep it to life eternal"* (John 12:25). Paul later said this:

> But whatever things were gain to me, those things I have counted as loss for the sake of Christ. More than that, I count **all things** to be loss in view of the surpassing value of knowing Christ Jesus my Lord, for whom I have suffered the loss of all things, and count them but rubbish so that I may gain Christ. (Philippians 3:7-8)

More loss. So, what happened to the "abundant life" that Jesus promised us in John 10:10? Loss and suffering do not sound like they are bedfellows with abundance. Could it be this "abundance" does not refer to possessions (which are "rubbish" according to Paul) or even happiness, comfort, or good fortune? Maybe our abundance will come in the form of character—character that is able to endure ill treatment from others, unfortunate circumstances, challenges with our kids, or even the open hostility of a culture that no longer values character, morals, or ethical considerations.

Maybe we will even begin to resemble Jesus, who was able to love the unlovable: prostitutes, tax collectors, et al. Paul was able to rejoice in his own suffering because he knew the endgame: living for Christ. Everything else he had (possessions, dignity, respect), he deemed expendable because he knew that his identity, value, self-esteem, and job (tentmaker) were simply means to an end: proclaiming Christ. The guy was completely sold out to his Master.

We "suffer" loss in many ways for many reasons, but the fantastic news about this form of suffering is this: If we are doing it in the name of Christ, understanding that our purpose in suffering is to glorify Him, then we are laying up for ourselves treasure in heaven where, as the Bible states, "neither moth nor rust destroys" (Matthew 6:20). This account full of "heavenly treasure" we are building with our Father is immensely valuable because, in the end, that is essentially what we will have to show Him on the day we finally enter His presence. Indeed, what we should really long to hear is God saying,

"Well done, good and faithful servant."

So, think of suffering "loss" not as a hindrance but as an investment that is accruing on your behalf. We want to go through our trials with such grace and forbearance that God is honored as our benefactor by all who observe us. What appears to be a problem in strictly human terms will hopefully be viewed by others as a demonstration of God's grace and provision and thus point others toward Jesus Christ.

As Christians, we are primarily here to glorify God. Hopefully that journey will include some happiness along the way, but there are no guarantees. Happiness may be a byproduct of a holy life lived out for the Lord, but it is not the primary objective. Most of us will find out that life is a mixture of sorrow and joy, with the sorrow not to be grieved over unduly, and the joy not to be taken for granted. After all, our true happiness lies on the other side of this brief physical life, which amounts to maybe 75 to 85 years if we're fortunate. But, the other side of this life is *forever*.

Think of being on the most beautiful beach you've ever walked on. Lots of sand there, right? The time spanning this physical life is equivalent to picking a single grain of sand off the surface of your beach and moving it 100 yards further inland. That would that take what…maybe three or four minutes, tops? The next life is equivalent to the time it would take you to move, grain-by-grain, **every single piece of sand** on your beautiful beach 100 yards inland. In other words, there's no end to the next life—it just *is*.

Exactly where we spend eternity is determined by the status of our relationship to Jesus Christ in this physical life. God tells us very clearly in the Bible that we must cast our vote for or against the Lord. Neither fence-sitting nor abstention is recommended because either of those options is a "no" vote in God's eyes. We are either for Him or against Him (Luke 11:23), and if you *are* for Him, it needs to be with both feet all in because if I understand my Bible correctly, He's not a fan of the half-hearted believer. In Revelation 3:16, Jesus says this:

> "So because you are lukewarm, and neither hot nor cold, I will spit you out of My mouth."

We are either all in or all out. Pay special heed to this warning if you happen to be a Sunday-only or one-day-a-week believer. Do you show up on the day, but God has no place in your life the rest of the week? You simply could be putting in an appearance. Unfortunately, there are many people going through that same routine, and they may be as far away from knowing the Lord as the neighborhood terrorist is. This is a wake-up call to those who see themselves in this description. God wants *all* of your heart. He accepts no substitute plans.

The all-in attitude is a must if we expect God to use us in other people's lives. In Mark 10:45, Jesus said this about Himself:

> "For even the Son of Man did not come to be served, but to serve, and to give His life a ransom for many."

God wants to use us as vessels to convey His love to others, but He needs our whole heart. Being like Jesus is not easy if we are trying to do it in our own strength. We need the power and presence only He can supply, so we have to be "plugged in" to the power source. The Apostle Paul is our prime example of staying connected; in fact, he was never *unplugged*, in the sense that he was willing to spend and be spent for the sake of others. He could do that because he recognized that God could be trusted to change anything in or about his life as the need arose. Whether that meant changing something inside of Paul or his outer circumstances was irrelevant because Paul remained connected to the Lord no matter what. What mattered to Paul was that God had unlimited access to his time and resources.

In his book, *Sacred Marriage: What If God Designed Marriage to Make Us Holy More Than to Make Us Happy?*, Gary Thomas puts forth the theory that the purpose of marriage is not to make us happy but to make us holy.[22] If we extend that theory to life as a whole, then what are the implications for us? They are far-reaching, for that means we must live as though God is after something much greater than a feel-good experience. He wants so much more for us! That should affect how we respond to people and problems.

We should strive to come through the fires in our lives as Daniel (Old Testament) and his friends did, exiting the fiery furnace not smelling of smoke and completely unharmed. In one sense, our lives are proof of God's love in that we, being the object of His love, are living monuments to His grace and care.

We may look a little roughed up, a bit worn in some places, but hopefully our character will reflect Christ to others.

Epilogue

I'M NOT SURE who will read these thoughts on some of the big questions, but please understand that I offer them not as an authority on these subjects but as something more akin to this:

> "Christianity is one beggar telling another beggar where he found bread."
> - D.T. Niles, New York Times, May 11, 1986

I grew up in the counterculture of the 1970s and was, by default, a skeptic where God was concerned. The only time I can remember even thinking about God was when I complained and used His Name in certain slang expressions, all of which I'm certain you already know. It never occurred to me that there might actually be a God who created us for the purpose of having a *relationship* with Him. I was merely meandering and partying my way through life, thinking I was on my own, until one spring day in 1982 when I had an encounter with Jesus Christ.

Fortunately, on that day, I was not drunk. I was not high. I was not depressed, nor was I manic. I was absolutely in my right mind when Jesus Christ supernaturally entered my being and changed my life forever. The brief religious training I had received in the Presbyterian Church as a young boy had not prepared me for this encounter with **the living God**. In fact, my whole concept of "religion" went right out the window that day because this was so much more than religion. This was intense, indescribable joy…this was *transformation*. I was the most surprised person on the face of the earth to discover that God was really there—and actually interacting with me. I was living the experience described in 2 Corinthians 5:17. I was a new person.

I was grateful afterwards to find my experience described

in copious detail in a book called *The Holy Bible*. I knew then that the God of the Bible was the same God who had contacted me and introduced Himself to me that day. I have spent the past 35 or so years cultivating this relationship with God, and along the way I have fallen in love with Him, with this God who set the moon and stars in their places, but who is also capable of maintaining an intimate, interactive relationship with any individual willing to make the effort to communicate.

So, I write these thoughts with hope that you will consider the possibility that God is actually *there* and seeking a relationship with *you*. I have found Him to be trustworthy, not without a sense of humor, and capable of loving me so well that I am occasionally reduced to tears trying to wrap my mind around what He has done for me. I can't wait to meet Him face-to-face one day.

I hope you will be there, too.

Draw near to God and He will draw near to you. (James 4:8a)

NOTES

[1] Keller, Timothy. *The Reason for God: Conversations on Faith and Life DVD Series*. Zondervan, 2010.

[2] Tolstoy, Leo. *The Death of Ivan Ilyich*. Various editions, 1886.

[3] Navigators, The. *Topical Memory System*. NavPress; Pap/Crds edition, 2006.

[4] "Tetelestai." *Strong's Exhaustive Concordance: New American Standard Bible*. biblehub.com/greek/5055.htm. Accessed 28 July 2017.

[5] "Salat in the Quran." *Quranaloneislam.net*. www.quranaloneislam.net. Accessed 28 July 2017.

[6] U.S. Const. "The Bill of Rights: A Transcription." *National Archives and Records Administration*. www.archives.gov/founding-docs/bill-of-rights-transcript. Accessed 4 April 2017.

[7] Kendrick, Alex, director. *War Room*. Tri Star Pictures, 2015.

[8] "James 1:8." *Barnes' Notes on the Bible*. biblehub.com/commentaries/james/1-8.htm. Accessed 24 April 2017.

[9] "Archegos." *The Hebrew-Greek Key Study Bible*, NASB edition. AMG Publishers, 2008.

[10] "Teleiotes." *The Hebrew-Greek Key Study Bible*, NASB edition. AMG Publishers, 2008.

[11] Chambers, Oswald. *My Utmost for His Highest*. Nov. 3rd reading. Dodd, Mead & Company, 1935.

[12] Peale, Norman Vincent. *The Power of Positive Thinking*. Simon and Schuster, 1952.

[13] "Quotes About Agape (30 Quotes)." *30 Quotes*. Goodreads. www.goodreads.com/quotes/tag/agape. Accessed 8 June 2017.

[14] "Summorphoo." *The Hebrew-Greek Key Study Bible*, NASB edition. AMG Publishers, 2008.

[15] Elliot, Elisabeth. *Shadow of the Almighty*. Simon and Schuster, 1958.

[16] The Urantia Foundation. *The Urantia Book: Revealing the Mysteries of God, the Universe, World History, Jesus, and Ourselves*. The Urantia Foundation, 1955.

[17] Lindsey, Hal. *The Liberation of Planet Earth*. Zondervan Publishing Company, 1974.

[18] Livgren, Kerry. *Leftoverture*, Don Kirshner Music, Inc., 1977.

[19] Boa, Kenneth, and Kerry Livgren. *Seeds of Change: The Spiritual Quest of Kerry Livgren*. Sparrow Press; Revised, Expanded edition, 1991.

[20] Lewis, C.S. *The Problem of Pain*. Macmillan Publishing Co., 1962.

[21] "Zadown." *The Hebrew-Greek Key Study Bible*, NASB edition. AMG Publishers, 2008.

[22] Thomas, Gary. *Sacred Marriage: What If God Designed Marriage to Make Us Holy More Than to Make Us Happy?* Zondervan; Reprint edition, 2015.

Bruce Hartley would love to connect with you via:

Facebook:

https://www.facebook.com/bruce.hartley.100

Email: hartleybruce@yahoo.com

If you appreciated what Bruce had to say, kindly consider leaving a review at Amazon or Goodreads.

Updates on future publications can be found at:

GROUND TRUTH PRESS

P.O. Box 7313
Nashua, NH 03060-7313

www.groundtruthpress.com

www.ingramcontent.com/pod-product-compliance
Lightning Source LLC
Chambersburg PA
CBHW031350040426
42444CB00005B/250